DREAMING THE MIRACLE
THREE FRENCH PROSE POETS:
JACOB, PONGE, FOLLAIN

DREAMING THE MIRACLE

Three French Prose Poets:
Max Jacob
Francis Ponge
Jean Follain

Translated by Beth Archer Brombert,
Mary Feeney, Louise Guiney,
William T. Kulik, and William Matthews

WHITE PINE PRESS • BUFFALO, NEW YORK

WHITE PINE PRESS
P.O. Box 236, Buffalo, New York 14201
www.whitepine.org

Some of the poems in this book are used by permission of
Editions Gallimard, Paris, France.

Publication of this book was made possible, in part,
by grants from the National Endowment for the Arts
and the New York State Council on the Arts.

Cover photo: Elaine LaMattina

Printed and bound in the United States of America

First Edition

1   3   5   7   9   10   8   6   4   2

ISBN 1-893996-17-4

Library of Congress Control Number: 2003100334

CONTENTS

Preface: The Prose Poetry of Max Jacob,
Francis Ponge and Jean Follain
by Peter Johnson · 13

MAX JACOB

Introduction by William T. Kulik · 21

FRANCIS PONGE

from *The Prairie*

Uncollected Poems

JEAN FOLLAIN

from *Canisy*

A World Rich in Anniversaries

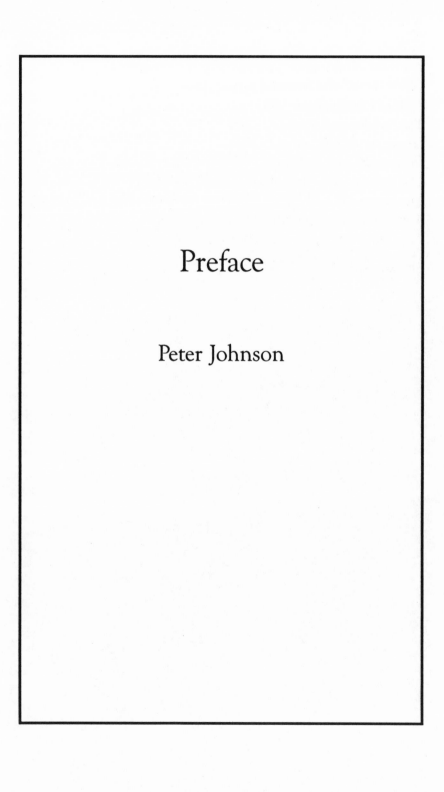

Preface

Peter Johnson

The Prose Poetry of Max Jacob, Francis Ponge, and Jean Follain

By Peter Johnson

It is impossible to discuss the American prose poem without focusing on a French tradition beginning with Charles Baudelaire (with a nod to Aloysisius Bertrand). More specifically, I have found it useful to view the prose poetry of various writers in relation to the prose poems of Baudelaire and Arthur Rimbaud—the former, arguably, a harbinger of the modern prose poem whose work has a high degree of referentiality; the latter, a harbinger of the postmodern prose poem whose prose poetry exhibits traits of what Marjorie Perloff has called "indeterminacy." Max Jacob, Francis Ponge, and Jean Follain form interesting links in a chain of French sensibilities which follow Baudelaire; and it is instructive for both readers and writers to see what each one of these writers brings to the form.

Each writer possess a unique way of "seeing." "Seeing comes before words," John Berger writes, and it is exciting to present such visions and sensibilities to see how these sensibilities enlighten each other and enlarge our notion of prose poetry.

"Let's distinguish a work's style from its situation," Max Jacob

wrote in his 1916 preface to *The Dice Cup*. "The style or will cre-
ates, that's to say separates. The situation distances, that is, it
excites the artistic feeling...." Later, he adds that the "prose poem,
to exist, must submit to the laws of all art which are style or will
and situation or emotion." When I speak of the peculiar "sensi-
bilities" of Jacob, Ponge, and Follain, I am, in a sense, referring to
Jacob's notion of "style" and "will," which he argues has nothing
to do with the way we normally think of style. "Language is mis-
taken for style," he writes. Instead, "style is the will to exteriorize
oneself by one's chosen means." Because Jacob insists that "An art
work has value in itself and not because it can be used for con-
frontations with reality," some critics have focused on his rhetoric,
seeing him as a proponent of "art for art's sake." Admittedly, it is
impossible to overlook his word games and puns, but it is also
important to recognize these verbal tricks as an extension of his
odd comic and satiric way of looking at the world. He is so irrev-
erent and playful throughout *The Dice Cup* that we are even forced
to question some of his statements in the "Preface." He suggests
that prose poets have to avoid "Baudelairean and Mallarmean
parables" if they want to distinguish their work from fables, yet
many of his poems take the Baudelairean ironic fable one step fur-
ther and end up undermining the entire. Consider a poem with
the title "Tale with No Moral." Or note the ironic sendups of genre
and discourse signaled by the unexpected openings to "A
Christmas Story": "Once upon a time there was an architect or a
horse: a horse rather than an architect, in Philadelphia, who'd
been told: 'Do you know the Cathedral of Cologne?'"; "Literary
Standards": "A dealer in Havana sent me a cigar wrapped in gold
which had been smoked a little. The poets sitting with me said
he'd done it to mock me..."); and "A Bit of Art Criticism": "Jacques
Claess is indeed a name for a Dutch painter. Let's, if you will, cast
a glance at its origins." Immediately, we have entered Monsieur
Max's world. The ambiguity in his poems reminds us of one of his
childhood journal entries. "Pain and voluptuousness are often so
close as to become one. Don't pursue this; it's one of those

thoughts that, with an appearance of depth, do not really mean anything at all." Yet it is precisely this ambiguity arising from the clash of opposites which surprises us in The Dice Cup and structures many of Jacob's poems, though perhaps "surprise" is not the best word. "To surprise is nothing," Jacob maintains in the "Preface." Instead, "one must transplant." Jacob's "will" or "style" not only transplants and grafts unlike images and discourses onto each other, but readers of his work also feel transplanted, caught up in his sensibility, which truly does "situate" his poetry. Jacob's effort to extricate himself from the shadows of previous prose poets does not seem convincing in the "Preface,"but, in the poems themselves, he becomes an original. There is a dream logic in his work, a kind of "logic of composition" that will later appear in the prose poems of Russell Edson and Charles Simic. After reading and rereading the poems in The Dice Cup, we truly feel as if we have been taught to "see" differently, to experience reality in an intuitive rather than an analytic way. Jacob trusts in his own imagination and in the imaginations of his readers. And seduced by his manic energy and swift juxtapositions, we trust him in spite of himself, knowing that behind his literary chicanery a true generosity of spirit lurks.

Francis Ponge has no use for Jacob's surrealist and cubist techniques and games, even though he frequented the company of surrealists for a time. His prose, restrained and sometimes painfully self-conscious, was inimical to the surrealists' belief in automatic writing. Although Jacob and Ponge both rely on puns and word play, they use them for different effects. Jacob is a jester *par excellence*, manipulating images and language to disrupt the strict forms and elevated themes of grand narratives, while Ponge is almost ascetic in his approach. As Martin Sorel writes: "A kind of mystic of the material world, Ponge wants us to look afresh at all that surrounds us, to respect and love it, so that there can be the proper and harmonious relationship between the human and nonhuman." Ponge himself writes, "It is clear that I am plant, a small branch, a leaf from one of the trees of those regions [of my childhood]."

In spite of their glaring differences, Jacob and Ponge are much alike in the way they privilege the role of the poet. At first, this statement may appear ludicrous. After all, in his "Preface" Jacob insists that any work of art "has value in itself." Similarly, Ponge argues over and over again for the need to efface the artist, so that language and object become one. Robert Bly restated Ponge's hope that a writer might be able to "describe an object or a creature without claiming it, without immersing it like a negative in his developing tank of disappointment and desire." But Bly, unlike Ponge, changed his mind and "no longer thinks that possible." And Ponge, whether or not he would like it, is everywhere in his poems—in his careful choice of language and in his playful irony in such poems as "Blackberries," "The Crate," and "The Candle." In spite of his well-known distrust of both ideas and of man's intervention in nature, Ponge's sensibility and intellect lurk behind his pretense for objectivity, especially in such poems as "The Pebble," "The Shrimp in Every (and All in a) State," and "The Goat," all of which merge theoretical discourse (sometimes for comic effect) and creative text. In fact, his presence is the perfect example of what Jacob calls "style" or "will," that special way of seeing and ordering (or disordering), which we graciously respond to in the best poetry. John Taylor argues that the "American poet begins with a fact and works toward an idea, while his French counterpart begins with an idea and works toward a fact." Maintaining that Ponge seems to see this difference in his preamble to "The Mimosa," Taylor goes on to say: "For Ponge, in other words, the objectifying poetic process, aiming at grasping the 'thing-in-itself,' must necessarily take into account the Cartesian *cogito ergo sum* as well as its logical consequence: 'Because I am, the outside world also exists.'" Taylor reminds us of the artist's inability to completely efface himself, and, ironically, it appears that the more he insists on his disappearance, the more he draws attention to his participation.

Some critics have compared Francis Ponge to Robbe-Grillet, but

Follain makes a better comparison because of the way he catalogues and slowly pans over images, avoiding cause-and-effect or explanatory conjunctions. Like Ponge and Robbe-Grillet, he strives for impersonality—in vain. "Close attention to things makes them seem strange," he writes. Granted, objects seem to act autonomously ("[chants go] up from every object"), and behind each thing often "a password lies hidden." But, again, the success of a poem depends on who is reading the passwords, who is listening to the chants, in short, who is recording the history of a "world rich in anniversaries." It is precisely because of Follain's original way of "seeing," his "generosity of attention," as Heather McHugh calls it, that his work astonishes us.

Unfortunately, not everyone has appreciated this quality of Follain's work. Reviewing a selection of Follain's prose poems, called A World Rich in Anniversaries, John Simon writes, "These pieces are bizarre, semi-nonsensical anecdotes or quaint catalogues of objects in a whimsical landscape or eccentric interior." Simon, of course, is responding to Follain's domestic scenes, subtle irony, and lack of apparent cause and effect. But none of Simon's generalizations holds up when we look closely at a poem from A World Rich in Anniversaries:

> On Easter Sunday the old man puts jewelry onto
> the wrists, ears, and neck of a long-haired woman.
> Already hitched to the black and yellow carriage,
> the glistening bay mare whinnies. A sailor sings by
> an engraving of the end of the world with Christ
> in the billowy heavens, the dead caught in their
> shrouds, leaving their graves. Time fills up with a
> future that may be fearsome. A child goes by on
> the road, wearing a motionless garter snake for a
> bracelet. How hot this long day beginning a centu-
> ry will be! Housebound, a deformed girl closes her
> blue eyes.

Follain merges the quotidian with the historical and somehow
stretches their union over a huge mythological canvas. The poem
begins with a catalogue of images, then turns toward the histori-
cal and eschatological with the "engraving of the end of the
world." With the introduction of "Time," the poem veers again
toward the historical, only to shift back to the present with the
image of the child walking down a road wearing a garter snake for
a bracelet. The word "motionless" is very important, suggesting
that time momentarily stops. But Follain's is the time of fairy tales;
his history occurs in the eternal present. "How hot this long day
beginning a century will be," he writes, then leaps to the image of
the housebound girl, which in its matter-of-fact eeriness comments
on the entire poem. Follain trades imagistic leaps for the com-
plexities inherent of the line break. More important, on a struc-
tural level, the final image of the "deformed girl" reminds us of
what Follain says occurs when a common "vocable" or "object"
appear in a poem. "The poem can be generated," he writes, "by
the sight of a simple object, never before seen in such a way, bearer
of all of its significant values and touching off a poem. The object
thus seen appears in its complexity with the rest of the universe
and situated in that universe."

It is true, then, that "Seeing comes before words," and that
foundations of poetic sensibilities are probably formed before lan-
guage acquisition. Yet it is with words that poets render these sen-
sibilities. A certain obsessiveness associated with genius must be
at work in Jacob's word play, Ponge's etymological games and Zen-
like devotion to objects, in Follain's humble and patient attention
to daily experience. Each poet, in his own peculiar way, works with
the raw material of the world, yet seems most attentive to what
Baudelaire called "the lyrical impulses of the soul, the undulations
of reverie, the jibes of conscience." This collection of prose poems
from Jacob, Ponge, and Follain finally gives us the chance to view
their geniuses side-by-side and to see them as part of an ever-evolv-
ing tradition of prose poetry.

Max Jacob
1876-1944

Translated
and with an introduction by
William T. Kulik

By the time he was fifty-five, Max Jacob (1876–1944) had become a bona fide literary lion, living in comfort at the Hotel Nollet, where he entertained established poets, painters and musicians as well as young, shy novices, all of whom had come for a taste of his brilliant conversation. Now tagged "the Picasso of poetry" and "renewer of the prose poem," a Chevalier de la légion d'honneur overseeing new editions of early works; he was a far cry from the Max who'd arrived in Paris at the turn of the last century to become an artist, working at menial daytime jobs—attorney's clerk, accompanist to a would-be La Scala star, freelance art critic ("because everyone was doing it," he said)—and taking classes at night. How, then, did a painter of middling talent set out on the road to becoming one of the great prose poets of the century? Picasso! Introduced by a mutual friend, Max and Pablo hit it off right away: the twenty-one year-old Spaniard, his work just beginning to be known; the twenty-five-year-old *plouc*, the hick from Brittany, awed instantly by Picasso's supreme self-confidence. So much so that when Max read him the poems he'd been secretly writing, and Pablo, though he knew almost no French, declared he was France's greatest poet, Max was charmed, insisting to the end of his life that if it hadn't been for Picasso's enthusiasm, he would never have become a writer. (Just as, in his vanity, he always wondered whether Pablo had urged him to give up painting and devote himself to poetry as a way of getting rid of a competitor!)

Soon they were inseparable and miserably poor ("like two lost children," Max said) both so depressed they once considered leaping off the balcony of their apartment. Their lives diverged when Picasso's paintings began to make him wealthy and famous while Max's work had come to nothing and he'd hit absolute bottom as a sales clerk for a cruel boss who taunted him and made him sweep floors and dump trash. He was depressed, humiliated, alone.

Which is how Pablo found him when he returned after a long visit home to set up at the Bateau-Lavoir, 13 rue Ravignan, later to become famous as—in Max's words—"the Central Laboratory for artistic experiment." Picasso practically ordered him to shave his

beard, quit his awful job and write. As he always would, Max felt
Picasso's power irresistible. He, "the poor little Jew who doesn't
believe he's a poet," moved to number 7, a hole in the wall, climb-
ing the hill every day to work side by side with his "terrible and
charming prince who reigned on Butte Montmartre." Then
Apollinaire came on the scene: brilliant, ebullient, cynosure of the
spirit of revolt against all received ideas about painting and poetry.
For the three of them, the core of the Modernist avant-garde, it was
art and nothing but.

Though Cubism is often said to have begun with *Les demoiselles
d'Avignon*, it had in fact been in progress since the earliest days of
experimentation at the Bateau-Lavoir with Picasso its chief expo-
nent. But, as John Berger has said: [though] "Cubism as a style
was created by painters, its spirit and confidence were maintained
by poets," especially Apollinaire and Jacob. Max, for example,
claimed he'd been "writing Cubist" since 1903, though his
groundbreaking work *Le cornet à dés/The Dice Cup* wasn't pub-
lished until 1917. With virtually no antecedents in the history of
the prose poem, inspired by, if anything, Mallarme's experiments
in *Un coup de dés*, in which chance elements were used to create a
poetry of words rather than a poetry of feelings, *The Dice Cup*
established Max as the "renewer" of the prose poem. Each of these
little "objects," one paragraph to no more than a page-and-a-half
long, has a clarity and resonance that results from the careful
placement of images that have been "worked" the way Picasso said
a Cubist painting must be: "only by allusion to reality." Like
Picasso, like Apollinaire, Braque and Gris, he disavowed "natural-
ism, realism, and every other work which has value only by com-
parison with the real." In the manifesto masquerading as a pref-
ace, Max speaks of elements "transplanted" from reality and "sit-
uated." Elsewhere he says that he never "felt more Cubist" than
when he arrived at the autonomous, self-contained reality , the par-
allel universe of this new prose poem "by means of the unreal"—
ordinary reality "bent" by the power of imagination to suit his
needs.

Like much Modernist painting , the purpose of this new kind of poem was to insist on the freedom of the artist to recreate the world according to his unique vision of it. To Max, that meant the freedom to upset the predictable, comforting world of the reader and show him, in Michel Leiris' phrase, "a universe whose nether sides are enchanted" in order to frustrate his expectations of a Good Story, one that confirms his reality by reflecting it. Instead, he aims at making crystal clear "the absurdity of our rituals and the things we hold dear." Often he does this through parody, mimicking the familiar, setting the reader up and knocking him down, sentence by sentence, image by image, luring him into "the little shock of doubt"—which Max considered the primary esthetic emotion—that creates the distance, "the margin of silence" between the poem itself and the reader's expectations of it. The result? A species of anti-poem, serious and not serious at the same time, a string of send-ups of familiar genres—biography, memoir, journalism, criticism, the novel, the fairytale, even the poem and, especially, The Literary Life (he loved Alfred Jarry's sarcastic line "It's as beautiful as literature"). All become "pseudo-types," all with "bent" elements of the real—bits of autobiography, real places and events, figures from history, myth and literature—"exteriorized" by a poet with the soul of a lyricist and the sensibility of a dramatist who confessed to having all his life "a comic opera in my belly." But in addition to that comic spirit—sometimes opposed to it, sometimes juxtaposed—a powerful mystic streak, an urge to express the ineffable.

Sometimes those little poetic jewels reflect light from a mysterious source, with images that sparkle like Venus in a dark sky, hinting at primal psychic truths. Because for Max, the philosophical ground of his prose poems is a belief in the truth of the language of the unconscious, but not rendered as a stream of raw data-the automatic or free-associated "direct transcription" of orthodox Surrealism. Instead, Max tried to replicate the eerie calm of the dream, the other-worldly glow of its images, their fantastic metamorphoses, their irrational, apparently random sequences: "I learned how to invent dreams," he said, in the shape of poems whose movement and content are based on the free-association of ideas, the only conscious mode that parallels the method of the dream. That he succeeded is underscored by the remarks of the critic Jean Cassou, writing in 1927, when Max's fame had been assured, to praise his achievement, calling him "the first to intro-duce the systematic use of dreams in literature," abolishing "all intermediaries between dream and reality."

If his professional life was a study in success, his bizarre per-sonal life was, as one psychiatrist has called it, "a real case study if there ever was one." Devils, angels, Christ-figures, all inhabit the poetic universe and the life of Max Jacob, Jew who turned Catholic after seeing Jesus on the wall of his room in 1909. "Split" is the kindest term to apply to a man who said he wished only to yield to the will of the God he claimed he loved and sought, but who often yielded instead to his impulse to homosexual seduction, orgy and the brain-bashing of ether. His anguished guilt over and fear of his uncontrollable behavior twice drove him to the Abbey of St-Benoît-sur-Loire. During his first stay he wrote a number of prose poems *(Visions infernales/Infernal Visions)* most of them expressions of his abject terror of the demons that filled his dreams—and his waking life. He struggled to bend his twisted will to the simple, orderly tasks of cloistered life: benedictions two times a day, wood-chopping, cooperation in the performance of daily household chores. In vain: the lure of the city was too pow-erful, and he returned to Paris to give himself one last chance at a decent secular life. The effort failed, and by 1934 he was back in the monastery for good. There he supported himself on book roy-alties and the sale of his paintings, his days filled with writing and entertaining a stream of guests (even Picasso, though they had grown distant with the years.) "Max the Nut" cloistered but still lionized! The prose poems of this final period vary widely in theme and tone: devotions, meditations, love poems; some are serious, some are written for a belly-laugh, to settle an old score, or chastise the unwary. Jean Follain, who knew him well in the

Nollet years, notes that Max "could switch in a flash from comic flippancy to painful seriousness," so that even mystical moments may be interrupted by a touch of the burlesque or by a detail from the ordinary—disparate moods juxtaposed perhaps to mock the conscious need for unity where none exists. Or, as some have cynically suggested, Max hiding true feeling "behind a series of verbal feints."

Many of these poems were written during the Occupation when Nazi doctrine made it clear that no apostate Jew was going to be treated as a Christian, monastic life or no, penitent or not, and Max became a prisoner, forced to wear the yellow star. Friends used what influence they had to free him (even Picasso, though Max's most loyal friends insisted he'd refused to help) and the daily flow of hopeful messages kept his spirits up. But after family members were seized one by one, imprisoned or killed, and it became clear he would not be released, his health declined and he turned his gaze away from the human world. He died in March, 1944, at the internment camp at Drancy.

WAR

Night: the outlying boulevards are full of snow. The muggers are soldiers; attacking with laughter and swords, they strip me of everything. I escape, only to end up in another square—is it a barracks square or an inn yard? All those sabers and lances. It's snowing. Someone sticks me with a needle: a poison to kill me! A death's head veiled in crêpe gnaws my finger. Dim streetlights cast my corpse's shadow on the snow.

Le cornet à dés

SEARCHING FOR THE TRAITOR

Another hotel! My friend Paul is a prisoner of the Germans. O God, where is he? At the Lautenberg, on rue Saint-Sulpice, a hotel with furnished rooms, but I don't know his number. The hotel desk is a pulpit too high for my eyes. I'd like to, do you have a Miss Cypriani...it should be 21 or 26 or 28 and me wondering about the cabalistic significance of those numbers. With Paul a prisoner of the Germans because he betrayed his colonel. What era are we living in? 21 26 or 28 are in white on a black background with three keys. Who is Miss Cypriani? Another spy.

Le cornet à dés

THE TRULY MIRACULOUS

Our dear old priest! After he'd left us, we saw him flying over the lake like a bat. He was so absorbed in his thoughts he didn't even see the miracle. He was astonished to find the hem of his cassock was wet.

Le cornet à dés

THE TREE-CHEWERS

Alone, imprisoned or at work, Dumas père consoled himself with the odor of a piece of women's clothing. Three identical men, same round hat, same short stature, were astonished they were so much the same and had come up with the same idea: to steal the lonely man's consolation.

Le cornet à dés

THE BIBLIOPHILE

The binding is a gilded wire-mesh imprisoning cockatoos of a thousand colors, boats with postage-stamp sails, sultanas wearing birds-of-paradise feathers to show how rich they are. The book imprisons very poor heroines, very black steamships and poor grey sparrows. The author is a head imprisoned by a great white wall (I'm alluding to his shirt-front).

Le cornet à dés

LA RUE RAVIGNAN

"You can't bathe in the same river twice," said the philosopher Heraclitus. But here it's always the same ones climbing the street. Happy or sad, they go by at the same times. I've named all of you who walk the rue Ravignan for famous dead people. Here's Agamemnon. There's Mme. Hanska! Ulysses is the milkman! Patroclus lives down the street! Castor and Pollux are the ladies on the fifth floor. But you, old ragman, who come to take the still-unspoiled scraps in the magic morning when I'm turning off my big good lamp, you that I don't know, mysterious poor ragpicker, I've given you a celebrated name: I call you Dostoevsky!

Le cornet à dés

THE BEGGAR WOMAN OF NAPLES

When I lived in Naples, there was a beggar woman at my palace gate I'd toss a coin to before getting into my carriage. One day, surprised that she never thanked me, I looked at her. As I did, I saw that what I'd mistaken for a beggar woman was a green wooden crate containing some red earth and a few half-rotten bananas.

Le cornet à dés

Success of Confession

On the road leading to the racetrack there was a beggar in servant's clothes: "Pity me" he said, "I'm depraved, I'll go bet whatever you give me." This is how his confession went. He had great success and he deserved it.

Le cornet à dés

LATUDE-ETUDE

A lot has been written about the case of Latude, but no one has told the truth. It was to protect herself from her own heart that Mme. Pompadour, that gracious Napoleon of love, had the little officer in his blue and white uniform locked up in the Bastille. Latude escapes! Where does he go? to the land of Spinoza. But he realized the taste for meditation is satisfied only in towers so he returned to his strongbox of love.

Le cornet à dés

THE JUDGMENT OF WOMEN

In hell, Dante and Virgil were inspecting a brand-new barrel. Dante walked around it. Virgil meditated. But it was only a barrel of pickled herring. Eve, still beautiful, lives here bent by despair even though she has the consolation of a halo for her nakedness. Holding her nose, she declared: "Ugh! That really stinks!" and drifted off.

Le cornet à dés

Poem in a Style Not Mine

for you, Baudelaire

Next to a holly bush through which a village could be seen, Don Juan, Rothschild, Faust and a painter were talking.

"I've amassed a huge fortune," said Rothschild, "and since it's given me no pleasure, I've kept getting more, hoping to find the joy that first million gave me."

"I've kept looking for love through all my misery," said Don Juan. "To be loved and not love in return is agony; but I've kept on looking, hoping to recapture the feeling of that first love."

"When I discovered the secret that brought me fame," said the painter, "I looked for other secrets to occupy my mind; but those secrets didn't bring the fame the first did so I've gone back to my formula, even though I'm sick of it."

"I gave up science for happiness," said Faust, "But came back to it even though my methods are out of date, because there's no happiness except in the search."

A young woman wearing a crown of artificial ivy appeared beside them saying:

"I'm bored, I'm too beautiful."

And from behind the holly God said:

"I know the universe, and I'm bored."

Le cornet à dés

A Christmas Story

Once upon a time there was an architect or a horse: a horse rather than an architect, in Philadelphia, who'd been told: "Do you know the cathedral of Cologne? Build a cathedral just like the one in Cologne!" And since he didn't know the cathedral of Cologne, he was put in prison. But in prison, an angel came to him saying: "Wolfgang, Wolfgang, why are you so sad?" "I have to stay in prison because I don't know the cathedral of Cologne." "You need Rhine wine to build the cathedral of Cologne. Just let them see this plan, then you can get out of prison." And the angel gave him the plan, and he showed them the plan and was able to get out of prison, but he never could build the cathedral because he couldn't find Rhine wine. He hit upon the idea of having Rhine wine shipped to Philadelphia, but they sent him an abominable French Moselle, so he couldn't build the cathedral of Cologne in Philadelphia; only an abominable Protestant church.

Le cornet à dés

METEMPSYCHOSIS

Here darkness and silence! with cloud-shaped pools of blood. The seven wives of Bluebeard no longer in the cupboard. All that's left of them this organdy headdress. But there! out on the ocean, seven galleys with ropes that hang down from topsail to sea like braids on women's shoulders. Getting closer and closer! They're here!

Le cornet à dés

A Touch of Modernism By Way of a Conclusion

In the ink black night, half the 1900 World's Fair drew back from the Seine and rolled over in one piece because a mad poet-head in the sky above the school is biting a diamond star.

Le cornet à dés

MYSTERY OF THE SKY

Coming back from the ball, I sat down at the window and gazed at the sky: it seemed to me the clouds were the huge heads of old men sitting at a table and someone brought them a white bird all decked out. A big river crossed the sky. One of the old men looked down at me, he was even going to speak when the spell was broken, leaving the pure twinkling stars.

Le cornet à dés

TALE WITH NO MORAL

Once upon a time there was a locomotive so kind she stopped to let pedestrians cross. One day, a car came bumping down her line. The engineer whispered in the ear of his mount: "Shall we file a grievance?" "He's young," said the locomotive, "and doesn't know any better." She confined herself to spitting a little contemptuous steam on the winded sportsman

Le cornet à dés

WHAT HAPPENS VIA THE FLUTE

The wounded traveler died at the farm and was buried under the trees on the lane. One day a rat crawled out of his grave: a passing horse reared up. But in his haste the rat left behind a half-chewed photograph. The traveler had asked to be buried with that picture of a woman wearing a low-cut dress. The rider who saw it fell in love with the original on the strength of the image.

Le cornet à dés

LET'S BRING BACK THE OLD THEMES

In a village where public sales of paintings are held in a courtyard, with frames right on the ground, the three-hundred-plus windows their owners had rented were crowded with butchers. It was like a public execution! Everyone there to witness the slaughter of art and happiness. Some of the butchers had binoculars.

Le cornet à dés

ERRORS OF MERCY

I'll go to prison with him rather than see him get away. And it was done! We're in a massive tower. One night in my sleep I reached out to restrain him and touched nothing but a white foot on its way to the ceiling. Now I'm alone here by a window in the tower. From the top of their massive haywagons the peasants gaze at me with merciful eyes.

Le cornet à dés

FAKE NEWS! NEW GRAVES!

During a performance at the Opéra of *For the Crown*, when Desdemona sings "My father is in Goritz and my heart is in Paris," a shot was heard in a box on the fifth balcony, then another in the orchestra and instantly rope ladders were uncoiled; a man climbed down from the top of the house: a bullet stopped him on the balcony level. The whole audience was armed and it turned out the hall was filled with nothing but...and...Then neighbors were murdered, jets of liquid fire. There was the siege of the boxes, the siege of the stage, the siege of a folding chair and the battle lasted eighteen days. Maybe the two camps were resupplied, I don't know, but what I know for sure is the newsmen all came for the grim performance, that one of them, being sick, sent his dear mother and she was deeply impressed by the sang-froid of a young French gentleman who held out for eighteen days in a proscenium box on nothing more than a little bouillon. This episode of the War of the Balconies did a lot for voluntary enlistments in the provinces. And I know of three brothers in brand-new uniforms, on my river bank, under my trees, who embraced each other dry-eyed while their families searched for sweaters in attic armoires.

Le cornet à dés

POEM

To erase the heads of the generals of the Empire! But they're still alive. All I can do is change their hats: which are full of gun-cotton, and these gentlemen of the Empire are not amused—gun-cotton is flammable. I didn't realize it was so dove-white. To enter that Biblical landscape! But it's a woodcut: a row of houses of different heights, a shoreline behind a trickle of water, a trickle of water behind a palm tree. Which is an illustration for *Saint Matorel*, the Max Jacob novel. Miss Leonie and I took a walk there; I didn't know people in that book carried suitcases! The generals seated at the table with the hats on were alive, but doesn't that mean Miss Leonie and I are, too? I can't enter that Biblical landscape, it's a woodcut–I even know the engraver. When their hats were back on the heads of the generals of the Empire, everything was where it should be. I re-entered the woodcut and peace reigned in the desert of art.

Le cornet à dés

LITERARY STANDARDS

A dealer in Havana sent me a partly-smoked cigar in a gold wrapper. The poets sitting with me said he'd done it to mock me, but the old Chinese who was our host said it was the custom in Havana when one wished to show great honor. I brought out two magnificent poems a scholar friend had written down translations of for me because I admired them when I heard them read. The poets said they were well-known and worthless. The old Chinese said they couldn't have known the poems because they only existed in a single manuscript copy in Pehlvi, a language they didn't know. Then the poets started laughing loudly like children while the old Chinese gazed at us sadly.

Le cornet à dés

A BIT OF ART CRITICISM

Jacques Claess is indeed a name for a Dutch painter. Let us, if you will, cast a glance at his origins. Little Jacques' mother, as she herself confessed, bleached her face with vinegar, which explains why the paintings of the master have a varnished look. In Jacques' village, on St. Roofer's Day, it was the custom of the roofers to let themselves drop from the rooftops without crushing the pedestrians; and they also had to throw their ropes from the sidewalk to the chimney. The whole thing very picturesque, which must certainly have given our painter his taste for the picturesque.

Le cornet à dés

UNTITLED

The glass case was such a deep shade of pink it might've been taken for mahogany. The jewels it contained had been stolen, then returned, but by whom? "What do you think?" my mother asked. I looked at the jewels: several clasps, some decorated with stones, others with tiny watercolors: "I think this thief's insulting us! He gives us back our jewels because they're worthless. I would've done the same thing." "That thief is an honest man," said my mother, "While you..."

Le cornet à dés

THE REAL LOSS

When I was young, I thought that genies and fairies went out of their way to guide me, and whatever abuse I took, I believed some-one was prompting others with words whose only goal was my well-being and mine alone. But reality and the disaster that made me a singer in the town square tell me I've been abandoned by those gods forever. Genies and fairies, give me back my illusion now

Le cornet à dés

PHILOSOPHICAL RETURN TO WHAT NO LONGER EXISTS

After adolescence, one may experience joy but not ecstasy. Using one shoe to hide the hole in the other, afraid you'll miss your train, just enough money for the trip and at the last moment your brother still half-asleep doubles it! Perhaps the ecstasy stems from the fact that restlessness and uncertainty are more agonizing when you're totally unaware. Should I have a love affair in Nantes? He who says "love" says gun, and I had no gun. But what surprised me most on this trip was being recognized at a shoe repair shop through my resemblance to an old relative and the praise I heard for that person whose life seemed to me worthless. Young people take everything seriously though they don't know how to give their seriousness to what they take. In fact, they bring to it only disproportionate emotions.

Le cornet à dés

THE TERRIBLE PRESENT

It was nothing but a Neapolitan crèche at Christmastime. Light fell on the coat of a doll with a fox's head wearing an overseas cap. That fox was questioning Oedipus condescendingly. "You won't answer me, Oedipus?" "Have you paid me to?"

Le cornet à dés

Hell Has Gradations

When I was working at the Fashion Cooperative I tried, despite the watchful eye of the dark, ugly old maid, to steal a pair of suspenders. I got chased down those splendid stairs not for the theft, but because I was a lazy worker who hated mindless finery. You descend, they follow. The stairs are less beautiful down by the offices than in the public area. They are less beautiful in shipping and handling than at the office level. They are even less beautiful down in the cellar! But what can I say about the swamp I came to? About the laughter? the animals I brushed against and the murmur of invisible things? The water turned into fire, my fear into a blackout. When I came to, I was in the hands of silent, unnameable surgeons.

Visions infernales

FEAR

Their giggling is horrible. They come down from the mountains yelling. They seem drunk, but they're not. I try to run but I know I can't. These dark men in masks are the worst, the end of every-thing! And the final torture: anyone who resists (is there a death more horrible?) is thrown into boiling water. And there isn't one consoling memory. Wake me from this sweaty, murderous dream. Wake me so I don't go to sleep again.

Visions infernales

WARNING

No light in the room! No door or window! He lies there suffering in every part of his poor body. No hope of any help, of the slightest relief. Not even that he'll die from his disease. No end to this pitch-black room, this unbearable illness, this howling like a woman in labor.

Visions infernales

THE BLOODY NUN

The confessional. The pulpit a bowl. Lidded chests and carved benches have been brought in, and while the surplice speaks using many persuasive gestures, the lids rise and fall and bloody eyes appear and disappear and greenish arms.

Visions infernales

BALLAD OF THE NIGHT VISITOR

What a winter that one of 1929 was! Paris in white velvet, all the windows like moonstones.

That night, that December night, I woke up in my cozy room in the Hotel Nollet with the wild reasoning of madness. In my cozy room, I dressed warmly in thick wool clothing because of the cold (it was about 2 A.M.) in good thick gloves and the wild reasoning of madness.

"Where are you going at this time of night, in the cold, darkness and snow?" asked the night watchman. "You'll never find a taxi." "I'm going to the Cirque du Temple, watchman." What a winter that one of 1929 was. Paris in white velvet, all the windows like moonstones, and every street: light and shadow.

"Let's go, my poor numb driver, 108 Boulevard du Temple, please." It was the only taxi running in Paris at that time of night in the pristine snow, at that pristine time of night. And how it had snowed! Then my feverish eyes, full of mystical apparition, gazed at your window, where you slept, I on a snow-covered bench and your window, your window like a moonstone.

"Are you a sleepwalker?" asked the driver anxiously, "because you don't look like a thief." Her house was before me with its window like all the windows: pearl, mica or moonstone. Then, in a dream or a smile, like an angel descended from paradise just for her, I went to touch her house—your gloves! take off your gloves!—then her door.

The taxi brought, then took back a man almost unconscious with joy, with the cold, with love, crying tears of joy, of love, of cold, of love, a man in tears.

"Already?" said the night watchman of the Hotel Nollet almost asleep that night. Whether it was a mechanical doll, a hypnotized victim...he climbed the quaint narrow stairs, decorated with a light switch...Whether it was I...or she in me...I don't know who it was: me? she in me? She, I saw her day and night, but not every day and night, and she knew nothing of that night visit at the white wall, at the oak door, in that Paris of white velvet and moonstone, light and shadow in every street...knew nothing of that visit.

After my love had died, O for long months after, the sorrow and the joy of having loved (do I still love you?), after the dark charnel house of bloody severing and you dead and I dead and you in me and I in you, and you dead and I dead, I here and you there, I spoke to you, my angel, I told you of my visit in the snow to your doorstep in that Paris of white velvet and moonstone, light and shadow in every street.

"I knew you were crazy because as any doctor will tell you, the really craziest are the calmest."

And you dead and I dead, and you in me and I in you, and you dead and I dead, I here and you there.

Ballades

IN CHINA

The Buttes-Chaumont painted on a screen, that's China. Every morning, four Europeans threatened with hanging are led to the gallows with great courtesy. Which is a rare occurrence. A house-maid pouring coffee looks at me more than at my cup: still she doesn't spill a drop.

The French ambassador and the muzzein vie with each other in silence and reticence. Everything here is neat and clean, a true paradise. It's all appearances.

Derniers poèmes

IF GUILLAUME'S DEATH HAD BEEN CHRISTIAN

And I'd been so sure he was going to die that through my tears I'd drawn him on his deathbed. I must confess I even had formal concerns. Next day he was walking around Paris, strong and majestic. One morning at Sacré-Coeur de Montmartre two big black cats squeezed me between them. A voice said "Don't be afraid!" Sacré Coeur looked like one of those pink fortresses that adorn the summits of Italian hills and he, Guillaume, high above, was like a bird with a man's head. Was he dead, our dear lyricist? My drawing wasn't finished. I bumped into him leading a group of disciples: was it he or Dante? Very much alive. Of course! Guillaume was not dead. A stout and clever priest said to me "There's no one more alive than Guillaume Apollinaire. But finish your drawing of his death and put a silhouette of <u>me</u> on the lower left-hand side."

Derniers poèmes

GRAVESIDE CHAT

Owing to I don't know what chain of events, the famous Mr. X. is here at the cemetery incognito. I'm the only one who recognizes and acknowledges him. Recognized, Mr. X. acknowledges the recognition, walks up to me to talk about my friend George. "He's here now because you left him on his own." "Oh, you know George. When he's got a nice fire, a good bottle of wine and a bad book..." "If you're speaking of your own, you're being much too modest." "George doesn't read my books."

Derniers poèmes

THE SOUL AND THE MIND

I remember that Malaysian prince whose body was only half-human, the rest black marble.

I remember the big rock and the miracle of my dreamy adolescence. Listen to this story, you who believe in miracles...Many serious people do, and I'm one of them. To believe in miracles, my serious friends, dispenses with the need to use the mind. In that era of curled hair and erect heads, I often went to the back of my father's property where there was a rock half-covered with moss and ivy. I always liked to stare at rocks and watch them come to life—even now I see figures and scenes at the corners of monuments and cliffs. At the back of my father's property!...

I sat down on the bench and stared at the rock, the moss and the ivy, and every time it was transformed in the same way. A camel! A real one made of stone, and on its back a stone Arab. Judging by his clothes, undoubtedly a prince. One summer evening,—my first back home for vacation—I went to gaze at the stone my eyes usually changed into a statue. I was very moved...to say the least...the camel was alive, turning its almah eye and pink neck toward me. The prince was still made of stone, sumptuously dressed in his usual foliage. Later on, I learned to regard such miracles as angelic warnings. When I reflect on the metamorphosis of the stone camel, I recall the Malaysian tale of the prince made of marble and flesh. The soul may advance without the mind following it.

Derniers poèmes

NOBLE OR COMMON

Those palace halls of legend were like the endless halls of hospitals. Before my birth or my deaths, I lived there, where everyone always spoke in hushed voices. There were two sets of hallways, one for the Lords, one for the common people. One might've confused them, if it weren't for holiday decorations: at which times the halls of the Lords had pots of flowers in front of each door corresponding to the church extravaganzas: red for the days of certain martyrs, white for the virgins, green and gold for Sundays. I remember I never knew what hallway I was supposed to use: common or noble. Who will tell me? The occasional gatherings of priests, nuns, or the great Lords, shall I ask them? Do they know me? And as for me? The parquet floors are a red lake of ice. And here's the attic: yes! just right for me.

Derniers poèmes

MIMI PINSON, OCTOGENARIAN

Poor woman, all her time spent in the country. How did she manage? "O what a beautiful lace bonnet." "I made that to keep myself busy, and this lace camisole." She opened her blouse and we saw that she had several little breasts, like a cat.

Derniers poèmes

THE PILGRIMS AT EMMAUS

I don't know who was there: it was one of those bistros where my youth vanished. A white marble table in the corner and the usual mirror that ran the length of the wall, turned and continued. I was wearing a ratty bowler and a look that questioned the sickly cast in the eye of the Lord. (Even though he looked more like John the Baptist it was really him!) "Since you're God and you know everything, tell me when this war will be over and," I added, "who will win." "You want me to tell you so you can become a barroom prophet?" He was silent. Night fell. There were no drinks on the table.

Dernier poèmes

CUSTOMS 1944

Right, I said, coming down that winding road from Penhars, just a little further and you'll find the chapel. A church in Breton Gothic style, torn down and completely rebuilt. Here we are! But my God, what a dirty trick! Instead of the comforting solitude of headstones above holy tombs, I see Marie Bidault her household and all her kitchen stuff!

Derniers poèmes

PRE-WAR

What crowds on Sunday evenings for those dinner-dances at the Colonnes! Look at the two drinkers getting up to dance. The bright hat of the accomplice is a pair of wings, and the lady vanishes with the rustling of a dove. Poor dear, am I supposed to pity you? The face of the dancer labels what he is, and the shadows between columns tell you where, through the smoky, ruined tables, he is leading you.

Derniers poèmes

THE CASTLE OF PAINBIS

Are you familiar with that proud castle at Chataignes in the Ayeron on the shores of the Lot, the castle of Painbis? The only person ever to enter it was M. Viollet-le-Duc, though lights have been seen at night and sounds heard. When historical monuments were the rage, 1820 or later, M. Viollet-le-Duc was sent to study the history of the castle, the castle of Painbis. He was met by a man in a turban, dressed Persian-style who said to him: "Monsieur, leave this place and tell no one what you've seen or you will suffer dire consequences." M. Viollet-le-Duc thought he should warn the police, who arrived in full uniform to make formal charges at the castle of Painbis. They were never heard from again. Some claim there was a window above the precipice that a human cluster flew out of into space. The castle of Painbis was not declared a historical monument. A century later, German troops who made the climb to the castle of Painbis retreated, vehicles and all, without anyone knowing what resistance they'd met, and their planes flew back to the sky without having bombed the castle of Painbis. Legend has it the man in the turban is immortal. Do you believe in angels, devils and everlasting ghosts? Where the body has fallen, eagles gather.

Derniers poèmes

SEVERAL JUDGMENTS BY OUR SET
WE CAN AMUSE OURSELVES WITH

Monday — "We had a good time yesterday at Melanie's: so delightful. Keep saying it so we'll convince ourselves it's true."

Tuesday — "How much fun we had yesterday at Suzanne's. Marcel's delightful but Anne-Marie's impossible..."

Wednesday — "We had a good time yesterday at Jules's. Let me emphasize that Maurice's paintings are charming, but Louis's music is worthless!—or so it seems."

Thursday — "Likewise."

Friday — "Likewise. Alfred killed himself. He was crazy. Yes, crazy."

Saturday — "Will we see you tomorrow at Augustine's? Max has gone to stay with the Benedictines. What a nut he was." "Yes, he's a nut. He has to be: a nut!"

Sunday — "He is a nut! Because, you know, a little religion is very *comme il faut*, but to push fanaticism to the point of going into retreat with the Benedictines is pure madness. Tell me, what does it look like to you? You know he..."

"Imagine that!"

Derniers poèmes

Town Crier

Lost: one beautiful soul, new condition, return to God its owner.

* * *

The river of my life is now a lake. Only love reflected in it: love of God, love in God.

* * *

There are stars that are bees, deep amber and onyx; others are bright sapphires. God has his eyes closed.

* * *

Today I see a town as just a pen and ink drawing or a dark curtain. Its roofs the peaks of gloomy moors. Yesterday I saw the country-side as a tapestry of moving silk.

* * *

When the rising sun had lit up the dark shadow cast by the tall-sided ship, we saw hundreds of fishing boats whose nets streamed with diamonds awakened by the dawn.

* * *

A wall! A mountain is a wall whose root is lost in terrible dark-ness. The wall is covered by hundred-year-old poplars with strange roots. Fireworks or another kind of blaze illuminates that great darkness and the poplars of glory were covered with blood.

Derniers poèmes

MY SOUL

Up on Butte Montmartre, before the dome of Sacré-Coeur, how many pagodas, temple idols, chapels, even monasteries. Not to mention apartment buildings, brand new and already demolished. Your white basilica rules now without contradiction.

And on Clichy Boulevard, how many women around the pushcarts who wouldn't dare tell who their men are! Even those wandering lost in this neighborhood: the pale little thing made anemic by failing her exams, the dignified lady with the haughty profile and all the others who bitterly regret being only flesh without a frame. You rule now without contradiction, Virgin with no other shield than the veil of Your Goodness.

Derniers poèmes

RECONSTRUCTION

All it takes is a five-year-old in pale blue coveralls drawing in a coloring book for a door to open into the light, for the house to be built again and the ochre hillside covered with flowers.

Derniers poèmes

Francis Ponge
1899–1988

Translated
and with an introduction by
Beth Archer Brombert

In the prose poetry of Francis Ponge, coming as he does in an unheroic age fashioned more by scientific than by classical studies, the direction is down rather than up, smaller rather than larger. The subjects of his allegories or fables belong to a lower world than that of the gods and heroes of antiquity and are treated zoomorphically, as opposed to the anthropomorphism of Aesop or LaFontaine. However, like his Renaissance antecedents, he too is creating a new humanism. He states his purpose to be "a descrip-tion-definition-literary art work" which, avoiding the drabness of the dictionary and the inadequacy of poetic description, will lead to a cosmogony, that is, an account—through the successive and cumulative stages of linguistic development—of the totality of man's view of the universe and his relationship to it.

Disclaiming any taste or talent for ideas, which disgust him because of their pretension to absolute truth, he abandons ideas and opts for things. Ideas, at least in any conventional philosophic form, are not for him. Since the truth they lay claim to can be invalidated by contradictory ideas, since there is no acquired capi-tal, no solid ground to step on or over, ideas remain in a state of flux, like the sea, and provoke in him a feeling of nausea.

There is nothing to count on, no truth to explain the whys and hows of our existence. But there is the melody, the work of art. In "My Creative Method," Ponge writes: "If I must exist...it can only be through some creation on my part," and goes on to explain what kind of creation he envisions. For Ponge, it is the word, in the singular, which reveals a life beyond its functional existence; a literary creation, yes, but a new form, a poetic encyclopedia that accounts for man's universe, and justifies the creator, through the many thicknesses of the word's existence, "borrowing the brevity and infallibility of the dictionary definition and the sensory aspect of the literary description."

However, it is not to be a hermetic form that exists for its own sake. Ponge is no partisan of art for art. The artist can proceed by many means to achieve his aim. But the end product, the art work, must be less concerned with mere narration or description of the object, be it a man, an event or a thing, than with the secrets it holds, the multiple notions behind it: "It is less the object that must be painted than an idea of that object."[1] It is 1922 and he still uses the word "idea" ingenuously. Warding off the anticipated accusation of "Romanticism!—it is nature we need instead of ideas, nature and her eternal traits," he replies:

> Where do you see them except in yourself, where can I see them except in myself? Nature exists—in us. Beauty exists—in us.[2]

The artist-creator, using nature as God used clay to fashion Adam, fleshes his bare creation with his ideas; clothes it in an artistic form, the chosen genre; uses his style to give expression to the face. This is where language, the form chosen by Ponge, becomes all important. Words are the raw material of poetry, containing in themselves a beauty which the poet can release, just as particular blocks of marble are both material and inspiration for the sculptor, the cut or grain of the piece suggesting its ultimate form.

In *Le Parti Pris des Choses*, the entrance gate to Ponge's domain, one sees these blocks of marble in miniature. The orange, the oyster, the snail, the pebble, are not merely described; they emerge as do figures from stone, characters from the novel.

Snails, trees, flowers, pebbles, the sea, all express an indomitable will, a striving for self-perfection, a single-minded purpose, that assumes heroic proportions, combining the excesses and self-mastery characteristic of the noblest of mythological heroes. Conquering the apparent futility of their acts, their vulnerability, their mortality, by continuing their efforts, they brave destiny by becoming more of what they are. "They are heroes," Ponge says in "The Snail," "beings whose existence is itself a work of art."

Beyond the connotation of option and will lies a more concealed and more complex implication in the arbitrary, partial quality of the expression as it is commonly used. Man, arbitrarily placed in the world, makes an arbitrary choice allowing him to survive in it before being arbitrarily removed from it, like the crate, used only once and then tossed on the trash heap. The poet, having chosen literature to make his life meaningful, uses words which can only partially convey his meaning, as his art, or the work of any man, can only partially express the man—or man the cosmos.

Although Ponge preaches phenomenology and accepts the label of "materialist"—which some of his admirers use to distinguish his work from the politically tainted literature of bourgeois humanism—he himself recognizes his debt to Rimbaud and Mallarmé who come out of an idealist tradition. And since the "thingliness" he practices does not function in a vacuum, he further recognizes that "everything written moralizes." It is in this connection that the allegorical nature of his poems appears. Insofar as these works utilize animals and things to point to a veiled meaning, they are fables. But they are not conventional fables, in that their purpose is not to moralize. They neither condemn immorality nor advocate virtue except perhaps in the sense of existentialist virtue, or the virtue of antiquity, both of which are self-achieved and self-discovered. They are perhaps more in the nature of a modern fairy tale, like Orwell's *Animal Farm*, which moves the reader precisely through its dispassionate tone, its absence of direct appeal. On the level of the fairy tale, Ponge is offering us a view of life transcribed into mute symbols, whose function is to "express (the object's) mute character, its lesson, in almost moral terms." However, unlike Orwell, he is not portraying man's incorrigible nature. Quite the contrary. He is showing us that the condition of life is mortality, but in death there is life: from the corpse of one culture another is born, carrying with it, through words, the chromosomes and genes of the past. The pebble, final offspring of a race of giants, is of the same stone as its enormous forebears. And if life offers no faith, no truth, it nonetheless offers possibilities. For trees there may be no way out of their treehood "by the means of trees"—leaves wither and fall—but they do not give up, they go on leafing season after season. They are not resigned. This is the first "lesson," the heroic vision, and the first weapon against mortality. The second is the creative urge, the "will to formation" and the perfection of whatever means are unique to the individual: the tree has leaves, the snail its silver wake, man his words. He also possesses all the "virtues" of the world he lives in: the fearful fearlessness of the shrimp, the stubbornness of the oyster, the determination of water, the cigarette's ability to create its own environment and its own destruction. The ultimate weapon is the work of art, the sublime regenerative possibility, which man carries within himself like the oyster its pearl, the orange its pip. These are not "morals" in any strict didactic sense, but they are lessons, of the kind that the Renaissance learned from antiquity—models of exemplary virtue to follow.

"The Prairie" ("*Le Pre*"), in that it incorporates all of Ponge's ideas, techniques, sensibility and eccentricity, seems to me his magnum opus. First published in 1967 in *Nouveau Recueil*, it was reprinted along with the journal Ponge kept during the four years of its composition and which provides the title, "*La Fabrique du Pre*" ("The Making of the Prairie").

Ponge's approbation, and appropriation, of nature; his awareness of himself as spectator and participant in an exterior world; his equally keen awareness of the reality of the verbal world of language, as valid and as external as the physical world, all reach their apogee in this poem. We see here concretized and poeticized the dual genealogies that run parallel throughout Ponge's work: the course of human, vegetable or mineral evolution, and its counterpart in the semantic history of words, the evolution of meaning.

The ultimate achievement for Ponge would be for each word composing a text to be taken in each of its successive connotations throughout history. This, were it possible, would be not just the tracing of language in a historical, philological sense, but the consecration of a birth to death rite which goes beyond the word to creation itself.

The creative urge, like the reproductive urge, is a movement toward death, in the sense of the self expended, and with the same goal: the birth of a new entity. The need to bridge the silence of mortality is the desire to fulfill one's function.

> The relationship between Eros and Thanatos is evident, and death in this sense is part of life. I have often insisted on the fact that it is necessary in some way to die in order to give birth to something, or someone, and I am not the first to have seen that the birth of a text can only occur through the death of the author. The sex act, the act of reproduction, also requires the presence of another. The two must die, more or less, for the third person, in this case the text, to be born. The second person for me is the thing, the object that provoked the desire and that also dies in the process of giving birth to the text. There is thus, at the same time, the death of the author and the death of the object of the desire—the thing, the pretext.[3]

In "Le Pré" the process is vividly metaphorized. Beginning with the emotion produced by the physical object, the prairie, he seeks to fix it, eternalize it, by writing it, for fear of losing it. His concern, at first, is merely to express it, render it, as would a landscape painter, using words in place of paint. The word *pré* itself soon becomes obsessive. It recurs everywhere, in every form; a simple phoneme whose implications far exceed its nominative function. Consulting the dictionary, Ponge discovers that "in fact, it is one of the most important roots existing in French.'"[4]

A certain graphic quality, arising perhaps from Ponge's initial impetus to render the prairie as landscape, is maintained throughout the poem, all the while moving out of nature into the works of man. Green is spread on a page, a small quadrangle, the words surging up from a brown page as grass rises out of the earth; a horizontal fragment of limited space, barely larger than a handkerchief, pelted by vertical storms and adverse signs, as the page, about the size of a handkerchief, is struck by vertical, horizontal and oblique signs of type.

And "did the original storm," the creative urge which rivals the divine, "not thunder" within the poet so that he would leave behind all fear and formality, and produce a truth commensurate with the objective reality, a "verdant verity" in which he could revel, having fulfilled his nature? "The bird flying over it in the opposite direction to writing" reminds him of the concrete reality which his poem only approximates, and of the contradiction inherent in the word *pré* with its multiple levels of meaning and time. And from the pleasurable image of a blue sky seen overhead while reclining on the grassy surface, he turns to the final rest beneath the same surface. Coming to an abrupt end, as does life itself, he places himself beneath the poem, through which his name will flower like the herbs above his grave.

There would seem to be no way out of ambiguity. Man cannot escape the ambiguity of his immortal spirit in a mortal condition, nor the poet the ambiguities of language by means of words. Even his chosen métier is ambiguous. He steadfastly refuses to consider himself a poet, or his writing poetry; at most he grants it the name of "prôemes." Yet these short pieces, even the ones on art, are undeniably poetic. He admits he "uses poetic magma" but hastily adds, "only to get rid of it." Just as he insists that "ideas are not my forte," yet ideas spring out of each page in dizzying profusion. And everything points to man—his formidable capacity for renewal, the glory of his mind and soul, albeit in a non-religious yet strongly metaphysical context. "The veneration of matter: what can be worthier of the spirit? Whereas the spirit venerating spirit..."

And so, he is a would-be encyclopedist compiling poetic language; a would-be materialist composing metaphysical texts in the least concrete of media; an anti-idealist who, like the plant that only uses the world as a mine for its protoplasm, digs into humanist culture merely for raw material, but evolves a neo-humanism combining classical techniques with romantic self-awareness; a fabulist who ridicules his moralizing; a Renaissance craftsman who uses modern science to fashion jewels—and all part of a search for beauty.

What Ponge is offering us is a taste of genuine culture, a synthesis of past and present, and at a time when sub- and counter-cultures are dulling our senses. Just as strings have been humiliated into making percussive sounds, and rhythms have been reduced to a hallucinating throb, so words have been simplified to the level of Orff instruments, limited to elementary meanings as are they to elementary sounds. In place of uniform bricks for factories, Ponge has unearthed varied material for palaces and temples, be they no larger than a snail shell.

And finally, he constructs a cosmogony which turns out to be an account not of the origin, but of the agony of the cosmos—an agony of joy as well as an agony of death. One has a feeling of eternal resurgence and surprise, each word like Chinese boxes opening one into the other, each text a fresh attempt to seize a fragment of the universe. If there is any graphic symbol to characterize Ponge, it would be the circle: the cycle of the seasons, the sea-rounded pebble, the orange, the plate, but above all, the circularity of his technique. He begins with the word, which inspires the form, which constructs the idea, which determines the word. In the beginning was the word, and in the end as well.

1. "Fragments Metatechniques," in *Nouveau Recueil,* p. 17.
2.. Ibid., p. 17.
3. *Entretiens de Francis Ponge avec Philippe Sollers,* Paris, Gallimard/Seuil, 1970, p. 171.
4. Ibid., pp. 172-173.

The End of Autumn

In the end, autumn is no more than a cold infusion. Dead leaves of all essences steep in the rain. No fermentation, no resulting alcohol: the effect of compresses applied to a wooden leg will not be felt till spring.

The stripping is messily done. All the doors of the reading room fly open and shut, slamming violently. Into the basket, into the basket! Nature tears up her manuscripts, demolishes her library, furiously thrashes her last fruits.

She suddenly gets up from her work table; her height at once immense. Unkempt, she keeps her head in the mist. Arms dangling, she rapturously inhales the icy wind that airs her thoughts. The days are short, night falls fast, there is no time for comedy.

The earth, amid the other planets in space, regains its seriousness. Its lighted side is narrower, infiltrated by valleys of shadow. Its shoes, like a tramp's, slosh and squeak

In this frog pond, this salubrious amphibiguity, everything regains strength, hops from rock to rock, and moves on to another meadow. Rivulets multiply.

That is what is called a thorough cleaning, and with no respect for conventions! Garbed in nakedness, drenched to the marrow.

And it lasts, does not dry immediately. Three months of healthy reflection in this condition; no vascular reaction, no bathrobe, no scrubbing brush. But its hearty constitution can take it.

And so, when the little buds begin to sprout again, they know what they are up to and what is going on—and if they peek out cautiously, all numb and flushed, they know why.

But here begins another tale, thereby hanging perhaps but not smelling like the black rule that will serve to draw my line under this one.

Poor Fishermen

Short of haulers, two chains constantly drawing the impasse toward them on the canal, the kids standing around near the baskets were shouting:

"Poor fishermen!" Here is the summary made to the lampposts:

"Half the fish lost flopping into the sand, three quarters of the crabs back out to sea."

Rum of the Ferns

From beneath the ferns and their lovely little girls do I get a perspective of Brazil?

Neither lumber for building, nor sticks for matches: odd leaves piled on the ground moistened by aged rum.

Sprouting, pulsating stems, prodigal virgins without guardians: an enormous binge of palms completely out of control, each one hiding two-thirds of the sky.

BLACKBERRIES

On the typographical bushes constituted by the poem, along a
road leading neither away from things nor to the spirit, certain
fruits are formed of an agglomeration of spheres filled by a drop
of ink.

* * *

Black, pink, khaki all together on the cluster, they offer the spec-
tacle of a haughty family of varying ages rather than a keen temp-
tation to pick them.

Given the disproportion between seeds and pulp, birds care lit-
tle for them, since in the end so little is left once through from
beak to anus.

* * *

But the poet during his professional stroll is left with some-
thing: "This," he says to himself, "is the way a fragile flower's
patient efforts succeed for the most part, very fragile though pro-
tected by a forbidding tangle of thorns. With few other qualities—
blackberries, black as ink—just as this poem was made."

THE CRATE

Halfway between *cage* (cage) and *cachot* (cell) the French language has *cageot* (crate), a simple openwork case for the transport of those fruits that invariably fall sick over the slightest suffocation.

Put together in such a way that at the end of its use it can be easily wrecked, it does not serve twice. Thus it is even less lasting than the melting or murky produce it encloses.

On all street corners leading to the market, it shines with the modest gleam of whitewood. Still brand new, and somewhat taken aback at being tossed on the trash pile in an awkward pose with no hope of return, this is a most likable object all considered—on whose fate it is perhaps wiser not to dwell too long.

THE CANDLE

On occasion night revives an unusual plant whose glow rearranges furnished rooms into masses of shadow.

Its leaf of gold stands impassive in the hollow of a little alabaster column on a very black pedicel.

Mothy butterflies assault it in place of the too high moon that mists the woods. But burned at once, or worn out by the struggle, they all tremble on the brink of a frenzy close to stupor.

Meanwhile, the candle, by the flickering of its rays on the book in the sudden release of its own smoke, encourages the reader— then leans over on its stand and drowns in its own aliment.

THE CIGARETTE

First let us present the atmosphere—hazy, dry, disordered—in which the cigarette is always placed sideways from the time it began creating it.

Then its person: a tiny torch far less luminous than odorous, from which a calculable number of small ash masses splinter and fall, according to a rhythm to be determined.

Finally its martyrdom: a glowing tip, scaling off in silver flakes, the newest ones forming a close muff around it.

THE ORANGE

Like the sponge, the orange aspires to regain face after enduring the ordeal of expression. But where the sponge always succeeds, the orange never does; for its cells have burst, its tissues are torn. While the rind alone is flabbily recovering its form, thanks to its resilience, an amber liquid has oozed out, accompanied, as we know, by sweet refreshment, sweet perfume but also by the bitter awareness of a premature expulsion of pips as well.

Must one take sides between these two poor ways of enduring oppression? The sponge is only a muscle and fills up with air, clean or dirty water, whatever: a vile exercise. The orange has better taste, but is too passive—and this fragrant sacrifice is really too great a kindness to the oppressor.

However, merely recalling its singular manner of perfuming the air and delighting its tormentor is not saying enough about the orange. One has to stress the glorious color of the resulting liquid which, more than lemon juice, makes the larynx open widely both to pronounce the word and ingest the juice without any apprehensive grimace of the mouth or raising of papillae.

And one remains speechless to declare the well-deserved admiration of the covering of the tender, fragile, russet oval ball inside that thick moist blotter, whose extremely thin but highly pigmented skin, bitterly flavorful, is just uneven enough to catch the light worthily on its perfect fruit form.

At the end of too brief a study, conducted as roundly as possible, one has to get down to the pip. This seed, shaped like a miniature lemon, is the color of the lemon tree's whitewood outside, and inside is the green of a pea or tender sprout. It is within this seed that one finds—after the sensational explosion of the Chinese lantern of flavors, colors and perfumes which is the fruited ball itself—the relative hardness and greenness (not entirely tasteless, by the way) of the wood, the branch, the leaf; in short, the puny albeit prime purpose of the fruit.

THE OYSTER

The oyster, about as big as a fair-sized pebble, is rougher, less evenly colored, brightly whitish. It is a world stubbornly closed. Yet it can be opened: one must hold it in a cloth, use a dull jagged knife, and try more than once. Avid fingers get cut, nails get chipped: a rough job. The repeated pryings mark its cover with white rings, like haloes.

Inside one finds a whole world, to eat and drink; under a firmament (properly speaking) of nacre, the skies above collapse on the skies below, forming nothing but a puddle, a viscous greenish blob that ebbs and flows on sight and smell, fringed with blackish lace along the edge.

Once in a rare while a globule pearls in its nacre throat, with which one instantly seeks to adorn oneself.

THE PLEASURES OF THE DOOR

Kings do not touch doors.

They know nothing of this pleasure: pushing before one gently or brusquely one of those large familiar panels, then turning back to replace it—holding a door in one's arms.

The pleasure of grabbing the midriff of one of these tall obstacles to a room by its porcelain node; that short clinch during which movement stops, the eye widens, and the whole body adjusts to its new surrounding.

With a friendly hand one still holds on to it, before closing it decisively and shutting oneself in—which the click of the tight but well-oiled spring pleasantly confirms.

FIRE

Fire has a system: first all the flames move in one direction ...

(One can only compare the gait of fire to that of an animal: it must first leave one place before occupying another; it moves like an amoeba and a giraffe at the same time, its neck lurching, its foot dragging) ...

Then, while the substances consumed with method collapse, the escaping gasses are subsequently transformed into one long flight of butterflies.

THE CYCLE OF THE SEASONS

Tired of having restrained themselves all winter, the trees suddenly take themselves for fools. They can stand it no longer: they let loose their words—a flood, a vomiting of green. They try to bring off a complete leafing of words. Oh well, too bad! It'll arrange itself any old way! In fact, it does arrange itself! No freedom whatever in leafing... They fling out all kinds of words, or so they think; fling out stems to hold still more words. "Our trunks," they say, "are there to shoulder it all." They try to hide, to get lost among each other. They think they can say everything, blanket the world with assorted words: but all they are saying is "trees." They can't even hold on to the birds who fly off again, and here they are rejoicing in having produced such strange flowers! Always the same leaf, always the same way of unfolding, the same limits; leaves always symmetrical to each other, symmetrically hung! Try another leaf.—The same! Once more.—Still the same! In short, nothing can put an end to it, except this sudden realization: "There is no way out of trees by means of trees." One more fatigue, one more change of mood. "Let it all yellow and fall. Let there be silence, bareness, AUTUMN."

THE MOLLUSK

The mollusk is a being...almost a...quality. It does not need a framework; just a rampart, something like paint inside a tube.

Here nature gives up the formal presentation of plasma. But she does show her interest by sheltering it carefully, inside a jewel case whose inner surface is the more beautiful.

So it's not just a glob of spittle, but a most precious reality.

The mollusk is endowed with a powerful force for locking itself in. To be perfectly frank, it's only a muscle, a hinge, a door closure with a door.

A door closure that secreted its door. Two slightly concave doors make up its entire dwelling.

Its first and last. It lives there until after its death.

No way of getting it out alive.

In this way and with this force, the tiniest cell in man's body clings to words—and vice versa.

Sometimes another being comes along and desecrates this tomb—when it is well made and settles there in the defunct builder's place.

The hermit crab for example.

SNAILS

Unlike cinders *(escarbilles)* which inhabit hot ash, snails *(escargots)* are partial to moist earth. *Go on** —they move forward glued to it with their whole bodies. They carry it away, they eat it, they excrete it. It goes through them. They go through it. An interpenetration in the best of taste, tone on tone so to speak—with a passive and an active element, the passive one simultaneously bathing and nourishing the active one, which displaces itself while it feeds.

(There is something else to be said about snails. To begin with, their own moisture. Their cold blood. Their extensibility.)

It might also be said that one can hardly imagine a snail outside its shell and not moving. As soon as it rests it withdraws deep into itself. On the other hand, its modesty makes it move as soon as it shows its nakedness, reveals its vulnerable form. It no sooner exposes itself than it moves on.

During dry spells, snails retire to ditches where the presence of their bodies apparently contributes to maintaining the moisture. There, no doubt, they neighbor with other cold-blooded creatures: toads, frogs... But when snails come out of the ditch it is not at the same pace as the others. Their merit in going in is much greater since getting out is so much harder.

Also to be noted: though they like moist earth, they do not like places where the proportion favors water, like swamps or ponds. And certainly they prefer solid ground, provided it is rich and moist.

They are also very partial to vegetables and plants whose leaves are green and water-laden. They know how to eat them, snipping off the tenderest parts and leaving only the veins. They really are the scourge of the salad patch.

What are they down in the ditch? Beings who enjoy it for certain of its attributes, but who have every intention of leaving it.

They are one of its constituent, though wandering, elements. And what is more, down in the ditch just as in the daylight of hard paths, their shell preserves their aloofness.

It must surely be a nuisance to carry this shell around everywhere, but they do not complain and in the end are quite satisfied. How marvelous, wherever one is, to be able to go home and shut out intruders. That makes it well worth the bother.

They drivel with pride over this ability, this convenience. "How do I manage to be so sensitive, so vulnerable a creature and yet so sheltered from intruders' assaults, so securely in possession of happiness and peace of mind?" Which explains that admirable carriage.

Though at the same time so attached to the earth, so touching and slow, so progressive and so capable of detaching myself from the earth to withdraw into myself and let the world go hang—a light kick can send me rolling anywhere. Yet I am quite sure of regaining my footing and re-attaching myself to the earth, wherever fate may have sent me, and finding my pasture right there: earth, most commonplace of foods.

What happiness, what joy then, to be a snail! But they stamp the mark of that proud drivel on everything they touch. A silver wake follows after them. And perhaps points them out to the winged beaks that have a passion for them. That is the catch, the question—to be or not to be (among the vain)—the danger.

All alone, obviously the snail is very much alone. He doesn't have many friends. But he doesn't need any to be happy. He is so attached to nature, enjoys it so completely and so intimately, he is a friend of the soil he kisses with his whole body, of the leaves, and of the sky toward which he so proudly lifts his head with its sensitive eyeballs; noble, slow, wise, proud, vain, arrogant.

Let us not suggest that in this he resembles the pig. No, he does not have those silly little feet, that nervous trot. That urge, that cowardice to run away in panic. Far more resistant, more stoic. More methodical, more dignified and surely less gluttonous. Less capricious—leaving this food to fall on another; less frantic and rushed in his gluttony, less fearful of missing out on something.

Nothing is more beautiful than this way of proceeding, slowly, surely, discreetly, and at what pains, this perfect gliding with which they honor the earth! Like a long ship with a silver wake. This way of moving forward is majestic, above all if one takes into account their vulnerability, their sensitive eyeballs.

Is a snail's anger noticeable? Are there examples of it? Since no gesture expresses it, perhaps it manifests itself by a more flocculent, more rapid secretion of drivel. That drivel of pride. In that case, their anger is expressed in the same way as their pride. Thus they reassure themselves and impress the world more richly, more silverly.

The expression of their anger, as well as their pride, shines when it dries. But it also constitutes their trace and signals them to the ravisher (the predator). And is furthermore ephemeral, only lasting until the next rainfall.

So it is with all those who unrepentingly express themselves in a wholly subjective way, and only in traces, with no concern for constructing and shaping their expression like a solid building with many dimensions; more durable than themselves.

But evidently they don't feel this need. They are heroes—beings whose existence is itself a work of art, rather than artists—makers of works of art.

Here I am touching on one of the major points of the lesson they offer, which is not by the way particular to them but which they have in common with all shellbearing creatures: this shell, a part of their being, is at the same time a work of art, a monument. It lasts far longer than they.

And that is the lesson they offer us. They are saints, making their life into a work of art—a work of art of their self-perfection. Their very secretion is produced in such a way that it creates its own form. Nothing exterior to them, to their essence, to their need is of their making. Nothing disproportionate, either, about their physique. Nothing unessential to it, required for it.

In this way they trace man's duty for him. Great thoughts

spring from the heart. Perfect yourself morally and you will pro-
duce beautiful lines. Morals and rhetoric combine in the ambition
and yearning of the sage.

But in what way saints? In their precise obedience to their own
nature. Therefore, first know thyself. And accept yourself for what
you are. In keeping with your vices.** In proportion to your size.

And what is the proper notion of man? Words and morals.
Humanism.

Paris, 21 March 1936

---

* In English in the original.
** The original edition of 1942 reads: "En accord avec tes vues.""The subse-
quent edition of 1949 reads: "En accord avec tes vices." I have opted for the lat-
ter.

THE BUTTERFLY

When the sugar prepared in the stem rises to the bottom of the flower, like a badly washed cup—a great event takes place on the ground where butterflies suddenly take off.

Because each caterpillar had its head blinded and blackened, and its torso shrunk by the veritable explosion from which its symmetrical wings flamed—

From then on the erratic butterfly no longer alights except by chance of route, or just about.

A flying match, its flame is not contagious. Furthermore, it arrives too late and can only acknowledge the flowers' blooming. Never mind: in the role of lamplighter, it checks the oil supply in each one, places on top of the flower the atrophied cocoon it carries, and so avenges its long, amorphous humiliation as a caterpillar at the stem's toot.

Miniscule airborne sailboat abused by the wind mistaking it for a twice-spawned petal, it gallivants around the garden.

MOSS

Patrols of vegetation once halted on stupefied rocks. Then thousands of tiny velvet rods sat themselves down cross-legged.

After that, ever since the apparent stiffening of the moss and its marshals against the rock, everything in the world—caught in inextricable confusion and fastened underneath—panics, stampedes, suffocates.

What's more, hairs have sprouted, with time; everything has grown more shadowed.

Oh, hairy preoccupations growing ever hairier! Thick rugs, in prayer when one is sitting on them, rise up today with muddled aspirations. In this way not only suffocations, but drownings occur.

Now it is becoming possible to scalp the austere and solid old rock of these terrains of saturated terrycloth, these dripping bath mats.

WATER

Below me, always below me is water. Always with lowered eyes do I look at it. It is like the ground, like a part of the ground, a modification of the ground.

It is bright and brilliant, formless and fresh, passive yet persistent in its one vice, gravity; disposing of extraordinary means to satisfy that vice—twisting, piercing, eroding, filtering.

This vice works from within as well: water collapses all the time, constantly sacrifices all form, tends only to humble itself, flattens itself on the ground, like a corpse, like the monks of certain orders. Always lower—that could be its motto; the opposite of excelsior.

*   *   *

One might almost say that water is mad, because of its hysterical need to obey gravity alone, a need that possesses it like an obsession.

Of course, everything in the world responds to this need, which always and everywhere must be satisfied. This cabinet, for example, proves to be terribly stubborn in its desire to stay on the ground, and if one day it found itself badly balanced, would sooner fall to pieces than run counter to that desire. But to a certain degree it teases gravity, defies it; does not give way in all its parts: its cornice, its moldings do not give in. Inherent in the cabinet is a resistance that benefits its personality and form.

LIQUID, by definition, is that which chooses to obey gravity rather than maintain its form, which rejects all form in order to obey gravity—and which loses all dignity because of that obsession, that pathological anxiety. Because of that vice which makes it fast, flowing, or stagnant, formless or fearsome, formless and fearsome, piercingly fearsome in cases; devious, filtering, winding—one can do anything one wants with it, even lead water through pipes to make it spout out vertically so as to enjoy the way it collapses in droplets: a real slave.

The sun and the moon, however, are envious of this exclusive influence, and try to take over whenever water happens to offer the opening of great expanses, and above all when in a state of least resistance—spread out in shallow puddles. Then the sun exacts an even greater tribute: forces it into a perpetual cycle, treats it like a gerbil on a wheel.

* * *

Water eludes me...slips between my fingers. And even so! It's not even that clean (like a lizard or a frog): it leaves traces, spots, on my hands that are quite slow to dry or have to be wiped. Water escapes me yet marks me, and there is not a thing I can do about it.

Ideologically it's the same thing: it eludes me, eludes all definition, but in my mind and on this sheet leaves traces, formless marks.

* * *

Water's instability: sensitive to the slightest change of level. Running down stairs two at a time. Playful, childishly obedient, returning as soon as called if one alters the slope on this side.

NOTES TOWARD A SHELL

A shell is a little thing, but I can make it look bigger by replacing it where I found it, on the vast expanse of sand. For if I take a handful of sand and observe what little remains in my hand after most of it has run out between my fingers, if I observe a few grains, then each grain individually, at that moment none of the grains seems small to me any longer, and soon the shell itself —this oyster shell or limpet or razor clam—will appear to be an enormous monument, both colossal and intricate, like the temples of Angkor, or the church of Saint Maclou, or the Pyramids, and with a meaning far stranger than these unquestioned works of man.

If I then stop to think that this shell, which a tongue of the sea can cover up, is inhabited by an animal, and if I add an animal to this shell by imagining it back under a few inches of water, you can well understand how much greater, more intense my impression becomes, and how different from the impression that can be produced by even the most remarkable of the monuments I just mentioned.

* * *

Man's monuments resemble the parts of his skeleton, or of any skeleton, with its big fleshless bones; they evoke no habitant of their size. What emerges from the greatest cathedrals is merely a formless throng of ants, and even the most sumptuous villas or palaces, made for only one man, are still more like bee hives or many-chambered ant hills than shells. When the lord leaves his manor he is certainly less impressive than the hermit crab exposing his monstrous claw at the mouth of the superb cone that houses him.

It may amuse me to think of Rome or Nîmes as a scattered skeleton—here a tibia, there the skull of a once living city, a once living citizen—but then I am obliged to imagine an enormous colossus of flesh and blood, which really has no bearing on what can be reasonably inferred from what we were taught, even with the aid of such expressions in the singular as The Roman People, The Persian Host.

How I would like someone, some day, to show me that such a colossus really existed; someone to support in some way my shaky belief in that phantasmic and singularly abstract vision! To be allowed to touch his cheeks, feel the shape of his arm, and the way it hung at his side.

All this the shell gives us: we are in full possession of it; we are never outside of nature; the mollusk and the crustacean are truly there. Which produces a kind of uneasiness that augments our pleasure.

*　*　*

Instead of those enormous monuments which only testify to the grotesque exaggeration of his imagination and his body (or his revolting social and convivial mores), instead of those statues scaled to him or slightly larger (I am thinking of Michaelangelo's David) which are only simple representations, I wish that man sculpted some kind of niches or shells to his proportion, something very different from the mollusk form yet similarly proportioned (in this respect I find African huts fairly satisfactory); that man used his skill to create over generations a dwelling not much larger than his body; that all his imagination and reason went into it; that he used his genius for adaptation, not disproportion—or at least that his genius recognized the limits of the body that contains it.

I do not even admire men like Pharaoh who used a multitude to erect monuments to only one; I would rather he had used this multitude for a work no larger or not much larger than his own body, or—which would have been even worthier—that he proved his superiority to other men by the nature of his own work.

In this sense I most admire a few restrained writers and musicians Bach, Rameau, Malherbe, Horace, Mallarmé—and writers most of all, because their monument is made of the genuine secretion common to the human mollusk, the thing most proportioned and suited to his body, yet as utterly different from his form as can be imagined: I mean WORDS.

Oh Louvre of the written word, which can perhaps, after the race has vanished, be inhabited by other dwellers, apes for example, or birds, or some superior being, just as the crustacean replaces the mollusk in the hermit crab.

And then, at the end of the whole animal kingdom, air and tiny grains of sand slowly seep into it, while on the ground it goes on sparkling and eroding, and disintegrates brilliantly. Oh sterile, immaterial dust, oh brilliant debris, though endlessly rolled and flattened between laminators of air and water, AT LAST!—there is no one left, no one to refashion the sand, not even into glass, IT IS THE END!

THE PEBBLE

A pebble is not an easy thing to define.

If one is satisfied with a simple description, one can start out by saying it is a form or state of stone between rock and gravel.

But this remark already implies a notion of stone that has to be justified. On this subject let me not be reproached for going even farther back than the Flood.

* * *

All rocks are offsprings through fission of the same enormous forebear. All one can say about this fabulous body is that once outside of limbo it did not remain standing.

When reason gets to it, it is already amorphous and sprawling in the doughy heavings of the death agony. Awakening for the baptism of a hero of the world's grandeur, reason discovers instead the ghastly trough of a death bed.

Let the reader not rush through this, but take the time to admire instead of dense funereal expressions—the grandeur and glory of a truth that has managed, whatever the degree, to render these expressions transparent yet not obscure itself completely.

This is how, on a planet already drab and cold, the sun presently shines. There is no flaming satellite to dissemble this fact any longer. All glory and all existence, everything that grants vision and vitality, the source of all objective reality has gone over to the sun. The heroes it engendered who gravitated around it have let themselves be eclipsed. But in order for the truth—whose glory they relinquish in behalf of its very source—to retain an audience and objects, already dead or about to be, they nonetheless continue to orbit around it and serve as spectators.

One can imagine that such a sacrifice—the expulsion of life from natures once glorious and ardent—was not accomplished without some dramatic inner upheavals. There you have the origin of the gray chaos of the Earth, our humble and magnificent abode.

And so, after a period of twists and turns, like a sleeping body thrashing under blankets, our hero, subdued (by his consciousness) as though by a gigantic straitjacket, no longer felt anything but intimate explosions, less and less frequent, with shattering effects on a mantle that grew heavier and colder.

Deceased hero and chaotic earth are nowadays confused.

* * *

The history of this body—having once and for all lost the capacity of being aroused in addition to that of recasting itself into a total entity ever since the slow catastrophe of cooling, will be no more than a history of perpetual disintegration. But at this very moment other things happen: with grandeur dead, life at once makes clear that the two have nothing in common. At once, in countless ways.

Such is the globe's appearance today. The severed cadaver of the being that was once the world's grandeur now serves merely as a background for the life of millions of beings infinitely smaller and more ephemeral. In places, their crowding is so dense it completely hides the sacred skeleton that was once their sole support. And it is only the infinite number of their corpses, having succeeded from that time in imitating the consistency of stone with what is called organic soil, that permits them of late to reproduce without owing anything to the rock.

Then too the liquid element, whose origin is perhaps as ancient as that of the element under discussion, having collected over greater and lesser areas, covers it, rubs it, and by repeated abrasion encourages its erosion.

I shall now describe some of the forms that stone, currently scattered and humbled by the world, offers for our examination.

* * *

The largest fragments—slabs almost invisible under the entwining plants that cling to them as much for religious as for other motives—make up the global skeleton.

These are veritable temples: not constructions arbitrarily raised above the ground, but the serene remains of the ancient hero who was really in the world not long ago.

Given to imagining great things amid the shadows and scents of the forests which sometimes cover these mysterious blocks, man by thought alone infers their continued existence beneath him.

In these same places, numerous smaller blocks attract his attention. Sprinkled in the underbrush by Time are odd-sized stone-crumbs, rolled between the dirty fingers of that god.

Ever since the explosion of their enormous forebear and their trajectory into the skies felled beyond redress, the rocks have kept silent.

Invaded and fractured by germination, like a man who has stopped shaving, furrowed and filled with loose earth, none of them, now incapable of any reaction at all, makes a sound any longer.

Their faces, their bodies are lined. Naivete draws close and settles in the wrinkles of experience. Roses sit on their gray knees and launch their naive diatribe against them. And they let them, they whose disastrous hail once lit up forests, whose duration in stupor and resignation is eternal.

They laugh to see around them so many generations of flowers born and condemned, whose coloring, whatever one says, is hardly more vivid than theirs, a pink as pale as their gray. They think (like statues, not bothering to say it) that these hues were borrowed from the rays of the setting sun, rays donned by the skies every evening in memory of a far brighter fire—that famous cataclysm during which they were hurled violently into the air and enjoyed an hour of stupendous freedom brought to an end by that formidable crash. Nearby, at the rocky knees of the giants watching from her shores the foaming labors of their fallen wives, the sea endlessly tears off blocks which she keeps, hugs, cradles, dandles in her arms; sifts, kneads, flattens, smoothes against her body; or leaves in a corner of her mouth like a Jordan almond, which she later takes out and places on some gentle sloping shore within easy reach of her already sizable collection, with the idea of picking it up soon again and caring for it even more affectionately, even more passionately.

Meanwhile, the wind blows making the sand whirl. And if one of these particles—last and smallest form of the object under consideration—happens to enter our eyes, it is in this way—its own blinding way—that stone punishes and terminates our contemplation.

Nature thus closes our eyes when it comes time to ask of memory whether the information gathered there by prolonged contemplation has not already provided it with a few principles.

* * *

To the mind in search of ideas which has first been nourished on such appearances, nature in terms of stone will ultimately appear, perhaps too simplistically—like a watch whose mechanism consists of wheels turning at different speeds though run by the same motor.

To die and live again, plants, animals, gases and liquids move more or less rapidly. The great wheel of stone seems to us practically, and even theoretically, immobile; we can only imagine a portion of its slowly disintegrating phase.

So that contrary to popular opinion, which makes stone in man's eyes a symbol of durability and impassiveness, one might say that stone, which does not regenerate, is in fact the only thing in nature that constantly dies.

And so when life, through the mouths of beings who successively and briefly get a taste of it, pretends to envy the indestructible solidity of its setting, the truth is it contributes to the continual disintegration of that setting. It is this unity of action that life finds so dramatic: it mistakenly believes that its foundation may one day fail it, while believing itself to be eternally renewable. Placed in a setting that has given up being moved, and dreams only of falling into ruin, life becomes nervous and agitated about knowing only how to renew.

At times stone itself seems agitated. This is in its final stages when, as pebble, gravel, sand, dust, it can no longer play its part as container or supporter of living things. Cut off from the original block, it rolls, flies, demands a place on the surface, and all of life retreats from the drab expanses where the frenzy of despair alternately scatters and reassembles it.

Finally, I would like to mention a very important principle, namely, that all forms of stone, all of which represent some stage of its evolution, exist simultaneously in the world. No generations, no vanished races here. Temples, Demigods, Wonders of the World, Mammoths, Heroes, Ancestors, live in daily contact with their grandchildren. Any man in his own garden can touch all the fully fleshed potentials of this world. There is no conception: everything exists. Or rather, as in paradise, all conception exists.

* * *

If I now wish to examine a specific type of stone with greater attention, its perfection of form and the fact that I can hold it, roll it around in my hand, make me choose the pebble.

Furthermore, the pebble is stone at precisely that stage when it reaches the age of the person, the individual, in other words, the age of speech.

Compared to the rocky ledge from which it is directly descended, it is stone already fragmented and polished into many nearly similar individuals. Compared to the finest gravel, one can say that because of where it is found and because not even man puts it to practical use, the pebble is stone still wild, or at least not domesticated.

For the remaining days without meaning in a world with no practical order, let us profit from its virtues.

* * *

Brought one day by one of the tide's countless wagons which seem to unload their useless cargo just for the sound of it, each pebble rests on a pile of its past and future forms.

Not far from places where a layer of loam still covers its enormous forebears, beneath the rocky ledge where its parents' love act still goes on, the pebble takes up residence on ground formed by their seed, where the bulldozing sea seeks it and loses it.

But these places to which the sea generally relegates it are the least suited to granting recognition. Whole populations lie there known only to the expanse; each pebble considers itself lost because it is unnumbered and sees only blind forces taking note of it.

In fact, wherever such flocks lie down they all but cover the ground completely, and their backs form a floor as awkward for the foot as for the mind.

No birds. Here and there a few blades of grass between the pebbles. Lizards scramble over them indifferently. Grasshoppers measure themselves rather than the pebbles with their leaps. Every now and again, a man distractedly tosses one far out.

But these objects of scant value, lost without order in a solitude broken by dune grass, seaweed, old corks and other debris of human provisions—imperturbable amid the greatest upheavals of the atmosphere—are mute spectators of these forces that run blindly after anything and for no reason until exhausted.

Rooted nowhere, they remain in their haphazard spot on the expanse. A wind strong enough to uproot a tree or knock down a building can not displace a pebble. But since it does raise up dust, the whirlwind sometimes ferrets one of these landmarks of chance out of their haphazard places, for centuries under the opaque and temporal bed of sand.

* * *

Water on the other hand, which makes everything slippery and spreads its fluidity to whatever it can encompass, sometimes manages to seduce these forms and carry them off. For the pebble remembers it was born of the thrusts of these formless monsters against the equally formless monster of stone.

And since its individuality can only be accomplished by repeated application of liquid, it remains by definition forever amenable to it.

Lackluster on the ground, as day is lackluster compared to night, the moment the wave takes hold of it, it starts to shine. And though the wave works only superficially, barely penetrating the very fine, hard-packed agglomerate, the very thin though active adherence of the liquid causes a noticeable modification of its surface. As though the water were repolishing it, thus assuaging the wounds of their earlier embraces. Then for a moment, the pebble's exterior resembles its interior; all over its body it has the sheen of youth.

Its perfect form is equally comfortable in either environment, remaining imperturbable in the sea's confusion. The pebble simply comes out of it a bit smaller, but intact, and just as great since its proportions in no way depend on its volume.

Once out of the water it dries immediately. Which is to say that despite the monstrous efforts to which it was subjected, no trace of liquid can remain on its surface; the pebble with no effort does away with it.

In short, smaller from day to day but always sure of its form; blind, solid and dry within, its nature does not allow it to become muddled by the waves, merely reduced. So that when vanquished it finally becomes sand, water can still not penetrate it as it penetrates dust. Keeping all traces except those of liquid, which limits itself to trying to erase all other traces, it lets the whole sea filter through, which disappears into its depths without in any way being able to make mud out of it.

I shall say no more, for this idea of signs disappearing makes me reflect on the faults of a style that relies too much on words.

Only too happy to have chosen for these beginnings the pebble: for a man of wit cannot fail to be amused, and also moved, when my critics say: "Having undertaken to write a description of stone, he got buried under it."

The Shrimp in Every (and All in a) State

The Shrimp Ten Times Summoned (For One Summation)

...Then from the depths of a watery chaos and a limpid density that can be distinguished from ink though poorly, I sometimes see rising up a tiny fearful question mark.

This little monster of circumspection, standing guard at the gates of his underwater dwelling, what does he want, where is he going?

Arched like a refined little finger, vial, translucent knick-knack, capricious vessel not unlike the capricorn beetle, vitreous chassis equipped with hypersensitive overanxious antennae, banquet hall, hall of mirrors, sanatorium, elevator—arched, cowering, glass-bellied, robed with a train ending in hairy paddles or coattails—he moves by jumps. Old chap, you have too many organs of circumspection. They will be your undoing.

I shall first compare you to a caterpillar, or a writhing gleaming worm, then to a fish.

Those stupid speeding bobbins, nibbling away with their noses in seaweed, will escape my sack more readily. Your organs of circumspection will detain you in my net, if I raise it fast enough out of the water— that environment unsuited to the unstoppered orifices of our senses, that natural washtub—unless by retrograde bounds (I was about to say retroactive, like a question mark), you return to the spacious recesses where the assumption—in unremembered depths, visionary heights—of the expert little diver takes place, as he spirals along, urged on by some vague impulse...

The shrimp, roughly the size of a knick-knack, has a consistency slightly softer than a fingernail, and practices the art of living in suspense within the worst marine confusion of the rocky hollows.

Like a knight on the road to Damascus suddenly struck by skepticism, it lives among its piled-up weapons, now wilted and transformed into organs of circumspection.

Its head under a helmet soldered to its thorax, generously fitted with antennae and feelers of extravagant delicacy... Endowed with the prompt power, residing in the tail, of a pack of unleashed hounds...

Standing guard at the gates of its underwater dwelling, almost motionless like a chandelier—by quick, jerky, successive, retrograde bounds, followed by quick returns, it escapes the direct onslaught of devouring maws, as well as any prolonged contemplation, any satisfactory ideated possession.

Nothing about it can be grasped at first, except that singular manner of fleeing which makes it seem to be some harmless optical illusion...

Assiduous, vulnerable...

First: circumstances. It lives in the worst marine confusion, in an environment inimical to our senses.

Second: quality. It is translucent.

Third: quality. It is encumbered by a profusion of hypersensitive organs of circumspection which cause it to jump backward on slightest contact.

Distinguished denizen of marine confusion, a transparency as useful as the way it jumps eliminates all continuity from its presence, even when immobile under scrutiny.

First: the shrimp's jump, cinematic theme. Stimulation of the desire for clear perception, expressed by millions of individuals.

Second: thanks to its not fleeing but haunting character, one slowly begins to grasp the following:

Third: a strange-looking knight whose wilted weapons have become instruments of calculation and circumspection. Conquest through inquest.

Fourth: but there's the rub—too many organs of circumspection lead it to its doom.

Revelation through death. A rosy death for the few elect.

Each shrimp has a million chances of a gray death in the mouth or gullet of some fish...

But a few elect, graced by the artificial elevation of their environmental temperature, experience a revealing death, a rosy death.

The shrimp's revealer is its cooking water.

Long ago perhaps, these animals, trusting their many weapons, enjoyed noble confidence...

We do not know what great fright or deception made them become so fearful.

Still, they have not yet taken to running away with their back turned.

They back away, always facing forward.

Helmeted, bearing a lance, like a tiny Athena,
proud and pusillanimous, skittish but steadfast,
between two rocks, between two pools,
amid whirling waters,
it emerges fully armed;
it sets off in conquest, in inquest...
But it has too many organs of circumspection.
They will betray it.

Pursued by fate or hunted by his enemies, a god, once among other gods, named Palaemon, entered the seas and was adopted by them: evolved galley, animal its own slave, gilled quinquereme without a crew.

Standing guard at the gates of its underwater dwelling, silent shipwreck, almost dead, full-rigged at all times, it feels out its freedom.

Then, amid the whirlings of icy waters in the hollows of the rocks' gaping skulls, what vague impulse urges it to expose itself, fearful little diver, summoned perhaps merely by a staring glance?

Body arched always ready to jump backward, it moves forward slowly, constantly pursuing its meticulous inquest.

Its head in a helmet soldered to its thorax, to which its abdomen is jointed, both compressed into a carapace, but a vitreous flexible one,

Chewing legs, walking legs, swimming legs, feelers, antennae, antennules: in all nineteen pairs of specialized appendages,

Anachronistic vessel, you have too many organs of circumspection; you will be betrayed by them.

Those stupid speeding bobbins, nibbling away with their noses in seaweed, will escape my sack (of netting to make you confuse it with liquid) more readily, leaving me with nothing but a cloud of mud.

Unless jump by jump—backward, jerky, unforeseeable—like the knight's jumps in the jungle of a three-dimensional chessboard, you gain a temporary assumption into the spacious recesses of dreams, beneath the rock from which I will not rise that easily discouraged.

The shrimp looks like certain harmless optical illusions in the form of dashes, commas, other equally simple signs—and jumps around not dissimilarly.

It is the quick-moving, fast-swimming species of the genus represented in the lower depths by the lobster, the prawn, the spiny lobster and, in cold streams, by the crayfish.

But is it any happier? That is another question....

It is considerably smaller than those heavy vehicles, its transparency is that of a fingernail, the consistency of its covering slightly softer.

Equipped with hypersensitive antennae, antennules, feelers, chewing legs, etc., all its power resides in its prompt tail which authorizes jumps that fool the eye, and save it from the direct onslaught of devouring maws.

All the squares of the three-dimensional chessboard are permissible, by virtue of its varied and unforeseeable jumps.

However, those jumps are restrained; its escape is not very far; its habits condemn it rigidly to this or that rock hollow.

Hardly more mobile than a chandelier, it is the distinguished denizen of marine confusion in the hollows of rocks.

In an upper circle of hell, it is a being condemned to a particular damnation. It ceaselessly feels out its freedom, it haunts emptiness.

Equipped with hypersensitive and cumbersome appendages, it is rigorously condemned to stay there because of its habits.

Impressively armed, even to the smallest details, its consistency remains nevertheless softer than a fingernail.

Its flight is short, its jumps restrained, and it returns ceaselessly to those places where its vulnerability is tested...

A circle of hell: the hollows of the rocks in the sea, with its various denizens, victims of particular damnations.

The condemnation of a being, in this environment of the worst marine confusion, in the hollows of rocks.

What vague impulse makes you leave these shores, carried off by the sea amid waves that ceaselessly and pitilessly contradict each other?

Equipped with antennules finer than Don Quixote's lance, dressed from head to tail in a cuirass, but of the transparency and consistency of a fingernail, its fleshly cargo seems to be nil...

Numerous qualities or circumstances make the shrimp the shyest object in the world, one which most successfully defies contemplation.

First of all, it appears most frequently in places where confusion is always at its peak: in the hollows of underwater rocks where liquid undulations ceaselessly contradict each other, where the eye in a limpid density barely distinguishable from ink never sees anything with certainty despite all its efforts.

In addition, endowed with hypersensitive antennae, it retracts on contact. Its jumps are very quick, jerky, retrograde, and are followed by slow returns.

That is why this superior arthropod is related to the kind of harmless optical illusions that are caused in man by fever, hunger, or simply fatigue.

Finally, and as effectively as those jumps which withdraw it to the least foreseeable squares of the three-dimensional chessboard, a useful transparency eliminates any manner of continuity, even when its presence is immobile under scrutiny.

...It blushes when dying in a certain way, through the elevation of its environmental temperature...

Nothing more expert, nothing more discreet.

A hunted god entered the seas.
A sunken galley evolved.

From the meeting of these two disasters
A beast was born, forever circumspect;

The shrimp is that monster
of circumspection.

THE SHRIMP EXAGGERATED

One can imagine no place unknown to you, flat on your belly, with your transparent insect-like roof, obtected by all the details of the universe, your vitreous chassis with its hypersensitive antennae that goes anywhere, deferential to everything, wise, exacting, fearful, orthodox, inflexible.

Shrimp of the azure depths and craggy holes, monster of the prompt tail that fools the eye; skeptical, arched, doubtful, fictive, shrinking shrimp, universally documented by an ever-searching periscope, but retracting on contact; fugacious, unobtrusive, stupefying nothing, no thrashing coelenterate tentacles, no plumes, floating at will.

Monster on the alert, on the alert for everything, on the alert for the discovery of the smallest parcel of sea floor, the smallest territory yet unknown to the commonest of strollers; watchful and calm, secure in the value, speed and accuracy of its instruments of inspection and calculation: nothing more knowledgeable, more discreet.

Mysterious chassis, framework of many things, stable, immobile, relaxed, indifferent to the cold movement of eye and touch, carrying around something like the narrow beam of a lighthouse in daylight, yet its passing is noticed, noted at fixed dates in the most deserted places—the beaches, the high seas of the earth, the inner theater of the rocks.

All the way to places where solitude, seen three-quarters from behind, walks on unaware of the glance that drinks it in, like a praying mantis, or any other phantom with a small head attached to a wandering body —aimless, but with seriousness and a certain fatality in its walk, wrapped in veils to keep its form imprecise.

Majestically, feeling the narrow beam of the lighthouse on the expanse, but without delay, impassive, ungrimacing, causing an indraft of nobility and grandeur, a sort of shadow or statue preceding me by only a few yards:

It could be a human being, a figure out of an allegory, or a grasshopper, though it does not advance by leaps and bounds, but by a steady walk, alternately placing its feet on the ground; the face, of which one only sees a vague profile, could be blind; its veils cloak it in such a way that the volume of its members seems greatly increased, the whole thing producing a constant waving or gesture intended to be followed by another.

Not only across swirling sands, but keeping fast behind, following with eye and step, with a feeling of respectful joy, without obligation, or sadness, assured of its mute protection,

its veils making it possible to follow it, to keep it in sight without having to overlook the landscape all the while maintaining its lead, its poise, never turning its head—a man, a child wandering along, unperturbed by the route he is forced to follow, nor by the pace maintained, nor even by the length of the walk,

who suddenly—on sitting down at the edge of the dune, which occurs as soon as fatigue has advised him to rest and give in to what is called taking stock of oneself—feels all sorts of gusts and puffs of delicious temperature on him, around him, holding on to his face, his ankles, his wrists and cheeks, during the assumption of the crayfish in azure depths.

ABODE OF THE GRAY SHRIMP

There, the wave, which returns to meet itself and is instantly rebuked and spat upon by its own family, retracts and admits its error. It falls into despair, displays its dishevelment, its self-made resolderings, etc.

(Absurd confusion of gravity.)

It is there, in the midst of constant remorse, constant upheaval of remorse (the opposite of bourgeois domestic life), of permanent repentance, it is there, where the swell persists, where cold broths are in commotion (whereas a perfectly reassured and reassuring pebble sinks to the bottom), that the shrimp is rigorously condemned by its habits.

It is there

In the churning waves

In the chilly broths

(also a consequence of the differences in temperature that start up, stir around, send off winds, and later, waves),

In the absurd confusion of gravity, playing against, struggling against other forces...

(the game: the clock game, to be precise; that is, an equilibrium slow to establish itself, which passes itself, repasses itself, etc....)

That is where, that is precisely where the shrimp, in order to live ...

(The fact that life is a chemical phenomenon also explains the confusion that characterizes it, the incessant struggle of conflicting forces. These things go together. Along with repentance. And regret.)

...is rigorously condemned by its habits.

It seems clear that the shrimp is aware of the confusion, the incessant contradictions of the environment in which it lives, while for fish it is dull tranquility: in no way are they bothered by these contradictory influences, nor does it seem they have to be aware of them.

If they are bothered by anything, it seems rather to be by the consistency of the environment, the heaviness of the air they breathe. One sees their mouths gaping, their eyes goggling. They seem to be living on the constant brink of asphyxia and resurrection.

Respiration for them is a complicated process. They have to dissociate the air in water. Most of their time is probably taken up with that, is spent on that. (At this point I am reminded of myself, spending most of my time trying to breathe economically: earning money. It takes nine hours a day... While for others, breathing comes so easily: for that, they have money in their pockets, that oxygen... But we, we have to work hard to extract money from work, from time, from fatigue.)

...But for the shrimp it isn't that at all. No. If it has a problem, it is not breathing, but stabilizing itself in the contrary currents that knock it against the rocks . . . And also fleeing, because of the cumbersome nature of its superfluous organs of circumspection.

(A problem that also reminds me of myself: we know others like that, in an era bereft of faith, rhetoric, unity of political action, etc...., etc....)

And so, while other forms—girdled, outlined by a simple, solid form—merely pass through these underwater lanes (these halls, rooms, alcoves) brightly, darkly, or sequined, in any event, opaque fugitives who will not return—following mysterious migrations as predetermined as the movement of the stars—the shrimp, almost immobile like a chandelier, haunts them, seems rigorously condemned to them by its habits. Its daring constantly brings it back to the very place its terror made it vacate.

With each rock hollow the shrimp forms a permanent esthetic unity (not only esthetic), thanks to its particular density and the transparency of its flesh; to the complexities of its contours which take hold there and become integrated like the teeth of gears; thanks also to the restrained jumps which keep it there (even better perhaps than immobility).

Like the first crystal formed from a liquid, like the first constellation born of a nebula, the shrimp is the pure Guest, the ideal Guest, the elect Guest, perfectly suited to this environment.

For it never stops exploring it, prospecting it, sounding it, examining it, feeling it, conducting a meticulous, fastidious inquiry about it, fearing it (fearing everything in it), feeling pain and anguish on its account, discovering it, haunting it; in short, making it habitable.

If on occasion it forgets the bonds of its nature and tries to rush off like a fish, it soon sees its error: there, and in that way, is the shrimp condemned to live...

It is the chandelier of confusion.
It is a monster of circumspection.
(Likewise, in troubled times, the poet.)

It must also be noted that the shrimp is the fleeting shadow, the form capable of fleeting—small, tenuous, good swimmer—among a genus represented in the depths by the spiny lobster, the prawn, the lobster, and in icy streams by the crayfish: all of them much heavier, bigger, stronger, better armed, more down to earth. The shrimp is like the translucent shadow, scaled down but miraculously just as concrete, of those enormous beings, those ponderous vehicles. But does that mean its fate is any happier?

Long ago, perhaps because of all its weapons, it may have enjoyed noble perfection and self-assurance, but after some unknown deception or great fright, it became extremely timorous...

The shrimp's jump: a sideways leap, unexpected, like the knight in the chessboard jungle; a leap that allows it to parry the attack of devouring maws. Jerky, oblique jumps.

Breaking away on contact, without however dashing out of sight (it is rather when the shrimp does not move that one loses sight of it), revealing itself thereafter in such a way as to raise doubts, not about its identity, but about the possibility of a study or somewhat prolonged contemplation of it, which might ultimately lead to some kind of esthetic grasp... Consequent arousal of the desire or need for clear perception... Shyness of the object as object.

Finally, however well-armed, however endowed with perfection, it still needs a revelation to become entirely confirmed in its own identity, and that revelation is known to few individuals among the species: through a privileged death, a rosy death, when their natural environment is raised to a high temperature.

The shrimp's revealer is its cooking water.

SHRIMP ONE

The worst marine confusion in the hollow of rocks contains a being the length of a little finger, about as hard as a fingernail, about whom nothing can be grasped at first except its singular manner of running away.

Endowed with the prompt power, residing in its tail, of a pack of hounds suddenly released—by means of rapid, unexpected, jerky, retrograde jumps, followed by slow returns, it escapes the direct onslaught of devouring maws as well as any examination.

A transparency as useful as the way it jumps further eliminates continuity from even its stationary presence under scruhny.

But fate, or compulsion, or daring, incessantly leads it back to the place from which its fright made it withdraw to begin with. Whereas other denizens, solidly and simply built, merely pass through these submarine grottoes as shadows or sparkles—as opaque runaways, in any case, not returning—the shrimp, virtually motionless, like a chandelier, seems rigorously condemned there by its habits.

It lies in the midst of its heaped-up weapons, its head under a helmet soldered to its thorax, generously equipped with antennae and feelers of extravagant sensitivity.

Oh, translucent vessel, indifferent to lures, you have too many organs of circumspection: you will be betrayed by them.

Those stupid speeding bobbins that nibble away with their noses in seaweed will escape from my sack more readily, leaving me with nothing but a cloud of mud—while you only achieve a temporary assumption in the spacious recesses under the rock from which I will not rise so easily discouraged.

SHRIMP TWO

Several characteristics or circumstances make a tiny animal one of the shyest things in the world and probably the most elusive object there is for contemplation; an animal it is less important to name right off than to evoke with prudence, allow to enter of its own accord (via pits and passages) into the conduits of circumlocution, and ultimately, to capture by words at the dialectic meeting point of its form, its environment, its mute condition, and the practice of its due profession.

Let us begin by admitting that there are times when a man's vision, upset by fever, hunger or simply fatigue, undergoes a temporary and probably harmless hallucination: from one end of his scope to the other, he sees a host of little signs moving in a particular way—in rapid, irregular, successive, backward jumps, followed by slow returns—indistinct, translucent, shaped like dashes, commas or other punctuation marks which, without hiding the world from him in any way, somehow obliterate it, move from place to place by superimposition, and finally make him want to rub his eyes so that by getting rid of them he can see better.

Now then, in the realm of external spectacles, an analogous phenomenon sometimes occurs: the shrimp, deep within the waves it inhabits, jumps around in a not dissimilar fashion, and just as the spots I mentioned above were the result of an optical disturbance, so this little creature seems at first to be the outgrowth of marine confusion. The shrimp is most often seen in places where even in calm weather this confusion is always at its peak: in the hollows of rocks where liquid ripples constantly contradict each other, in this pure density barely distinguishable from ink, where the eye never sees anything for sure despite all its efforts. A transparency as useful as the way it jumps eliminates all continuity from its presence, even when immobile under scrutiny.

At this very point it becomes imperative that blurred illusion, encouraged by doubt and difficulty, not prevail over reason; illusion by which the shrimp—because our thwarted scrutiny passes almost at once into memory—would be remembered as no more than a reflection, or the fleeting fast-swimming shadow of species represented more tangibly on the sea bottom by lobsters or prawns, and in icy streams by crayfish. No, without a doubt, the shrimp is just as alive as those clumsy vehicles and knows, though its condition is less down-to-earth, all the pain and suffering that life anywhere entails... If the extreme inner complexity that at times animates them is not to prevent us from honoring the more characteristic forms of a stylization to which they are entitled—treating them later, when necessary, as mere ideograms—then we must not allow this use to spare us the sympathetic suffering which the observation of life irresistibly arouses in us—the price, no doubt, of an accurate understanding of the animate world.

What can add greater interest to a form than the observation that its reproduction and dissemination throughout nature occurs in millions of copies at the same time everywhere, in fresh and salt water, in good weather and bad? Though many individuals suffer from this form and its particular damnation, wherever this phenomenon occurs we feel arise in us a desire for clear perception. Objects that as objects are shy, appear to raise less doubt about the reality of each individual than about the possibility of a somewhat prolonged contemplation of it, a somewhat satisfying ideated possession; prompt power, residing in the tail, of a pack of hounds suddenly tearing loose: it is probably in the cinema rather than in architecture that a theme like this can finally be used... First the art of living had to be seen to: we should have taken up that challenge.

1926-1934

THE PIGEON

Grain-fed belly, come down over here,
Saintly gray pigeon belly...

The way a storm rains, walks on broad talons,
Floats over, takes over the lawn,
Where first you rebounded
With the charming cooings of the thunder.

Show us soon your rainbow throat...

Then fly away obliquely, in a great flapping of wings that pull,
pleat, or rent the silken cover of the clouds.

1925

THE FROG

When little matchsticks of rain bounce off drenched fields, an amphibian dwarf, a maimed Ophelia, barely the size of a fist, sometimes hops under the poet's feet and flings herself into the next pond.

Let the nervous little thing run away. She has lovely legs. Her whole body is sheathed in waterproof skin. Hardly meat, her long muscles have an elegance neither fish nor fowl. But to escape one's fingers, the virtue of fluidity joins forces with her struggle for life. Goitrous, she starts panting... And that pounding heart, those wrinkled eyelids, that drooping mouth, move me to let her go.

1937

THE HORSE

Many times the size of man, the horse has flaring nostrils, round eyes under half-closed lids, cocked ears and long muscular neck.

The tallest of man's domestic animals, and truly his designated mount.

Man, somewhat lost on an elephant, is at his best on a horse, truly a throne to his measure.

We will not do away with the horse, I hope?

He will not become a curiosity in a zoo?

...Already now, in town, he is no more than a miserable substitute for the automobile, the most miserable means of traction.

Ah, the horse is also—does man suspect it?—something else besides! He is *impatience* nostrilized.

His weapons are running, biting, bucking.

He seems to have a keen nose, keen ears, and very sensitive eyes.

The greatest tribute one can pay him is having to fit him with blinders.

But no weapon...

Whereby the temptation to add one. One only. A horn.

Thereby the unicorn.

The horse, terribly nervous, is aerophagous.

Hypersensitive, he clamps his jaws, holds his breath, then releases it, making the walls of his nasal cavities vibrate loudly.

That is why this noble beast, who feeds on air and grass alone, produces only straw turds and thunderous fragrant farts.

Fragrant thunderisms.

What am I saying, feeds on air? Gets drunk on it. Sniffs it, savors it, snorts it.

He rushes into it, shakes his mane in it, kicks up his hind legs in it.

He would evidently like to fly up in it.

The flight of clouds inspires him, urges him to imitation.

He does imitate it: he tosses, prances...

And when the whip's lightning claps, the clouds gallop faster and rain tramples the earth...

Out of your stall, high-spirited over-sensitive armoire, all polished and smoothed!

Great beautiful period piece!

Polished ebony or mahogany.

Stroke the withers of this armoire and immediately it has a faraway look.

Dust cloth at the lips, feather mop at the rump, key in the lock of the nostrils.

His skin quivers, irritably tolerating flies, his shoe hammers the ground.

He lowers his head, leans his muzzle toward the ground and consoles himself with grass.

A stepstool is needed to look on the upper shelf.

Ticklish skin, as I was saying...but his natural impatience is so profound, that inside his body the parts of his skeleton behave like pebbles in a torrent!

Seen from the apse, the highest animal nave in the stable...

Great saint! Great horse! Beautiful behind in the stable...

What is this splendid courtesan's behind that greets me, set on slim legs, high heels?

Giant goose of the golden eggs, strangely clipped.

Ah, it is the smell of gold that assails my nostrils!

Leather and manure mixed together.

Strong-smelling omelette, from the goose of the golden eggs.

Straw omelette, earth omelette, flavored with the rum of your urine, dropping from the crack under your tail...

As though fresh from the oven, on a pastry sheet, the stable's rolls and rum balls.

Great saint, with your Byzantine eyes, woeful, under the harness...

A sort of saint, humble monk at prayer, in the twilight.

A monk? What am I saying?...A pontiff, on his excremental palanquin! A pope exhibiting to all comers a splendid courtesan's behind, generously heart-shaped, on slender legs ending elegantly in high-heeled shoes.

WHAT IS THIS CLACKING OF THE BIT?

THESE DULL THUDS IN THE STALL?

WHAT'S GOING ON?

PONTIFF AT PRAYER?

SCHOOLBOY IN DETENTION?

GREAT SAINTS! GREAT HORSES (HORSES OR HEROES?), OF THE BEAUTIFUL BEHIND IN THE STABLE,

WHY, SAINTLY MONK, ARE YOU WEARING RIDING BREECHES?

—INTERRUPTED DURING HIS MASS, HE TURNED HIS BYZANTINE EYES TOWARD US...

1948-1951

MANURE

Straw rolls, easily crumbled. Steamy, smelly. Smashed by wagon wheels, or spared by the breadth of the axle.

You have come to be thought of as something precious. Still, you are scooped up with a shovel. This shows human respect. It is true your odor would cling to the hands.

In any case, you are not beyond the pale, nor as repulsive as the droppings of dogs and cats, which have the misfortune of too closely resembling man's in their mortar-like pastiness and annoying stickiness.

1932

THE GOAT

And if hell is myth in the heart of the earth, it is true in my heart.
—Malherbe

To Odette

Our tenderness at the notion of the goat is immediately aroused because, between her frail legs, she carries around all that milk—swelling the bagpipe with its downcast thumbs which the poor thing badly hides under the rug passing for a shawl that always lies askew on her rump—obtained through the nibbled means of a few sparse herbs, or vines, of aromatic essence.

"Mere nibblings, you said it," they'll tell us. True, but tenacious all the same.

And that bell which never stops.

All that fuss, she chooses to think, for the grace of her off-spring, that is, for raising this little wooden stool that jumps around in place on four legs doing jetés until? Following his mother's example, he behaves more like a stepstool, placing his forelegs on the first natural step he can find, so as to graze even higher than what lies within easy reach.

And capricious to boot, headstrong!

However small his horns, he affronts anything.

"Ah! Those kids are getting our goat," they mutter—untiring wet-nurses and remote princesses, like the galaxies—and kneel down to rest. Head high, moreover, and under heavy lids a fabulous starry-eyed look. However, uncrucifying their stiff limbs with a sudden effort, they get up almost at once, for they do not forget their duty.

These long-eyed beauties, hairy as beasts, beauteous and at the same time bumptious—or better said, Beelzebumptious—when they bleat, what are they bewailing? what torment? what distress?

Like old bachelors, they are fond of newspapers and tobacco.

And in connection with goats, one should doubtless mention rope, and even (what pullings! what placid jerking obstinacy!) rope at the end of its rope, a rope whip.

That goatee, that grave accent...

They haunt rocky places.

With a perfectly natural inflection, psalmodizing a bit from here on—we too going a bit far to seize the verbal occasion by the horns—let us, head high, make it known that *chèvre* (goat), not far from *cheval* (horse), but feminine with a grave accent, is merely a modulated modification which prances neither up nor down but rather climbs, with its last syllable, up those jagged rocks, up to the take-off area, the aerie of the mewt *e*.

No galloping with that in sight, however. No triumphal leap. None of those bounds, halted at the edge of the precipice by the shudder of failure along the chamois' skin.

No. For having reached those heights step by step, brought closer and closer by her researches—and missing the point—it would seem she apologizes humbly, lips atremble.

"This is really not for me," she stammers. "I'll not be caught here again."—and clambers down to the first bush.

This, in fact, is how the goat most often appears to us in the mountains, or in those regions cast off by nature: clinging, ragged animal, to bushes, ragged plants, themselves clinging to ragged minerals—those jagged cliffs, crumbled stones.

And she doubtless seems so pitiful for being, from a certain viewpoint, no more than that: a faulty tatter, a tether, a miserable accident; a hopeless approximation; a somewhat sordid adaptation to contingencies themselves sordid; and in the end, nothing but shreds.

And yet, here is a machine—a model germane to ours and thus fraternally cherished by us; by that I mean, within the realm of vagrant animation long ago conceived and perfected by nature—for obtaining milk under the hardest conditions.

It may be no more than a pathetic and pitiable animal, yet still a prodigious organism, a being, and it works.

So that the goat, like all creatures, is both an error and the accomplished perfection of that error; and thus deplorable and admirable, fearful and fascinating at once.

And we? Surely we can find enough satisfaction in trying to express this (imperfectly).

Thus shall I, each day, have loosed the goat on my note pad: sketch, draft, scrap of a study, as the goat herself is loosed on the mountain by her owner, against those bushes, those rocks—those hazardous thickets, those inert words—from which she is barely distinguishable at first glance.

And yet, on observing carefully, *she* lives, *she* moves. If one approaches, she pulls on her rope and tries to flee. One need not press her too hard to draw from her at once some of that milk, more precious and fragrant than any other—smelling like the spark of flint, furtively suggesting the metallurgy of hell—but exactly like the milk of the stars splattered across the night sky by reason of such violence, and whose infinite multitude and distance makes of their light this milt—drink and seed in one—diffused ineffably within us.

Nourishing, soothing, still warm, ah, surely it befits us to drink this milk, but in no way take pride in it. Any more, finally, than in the sap of our words, so long destined for us, perhaps—by way of the kid and the goat—as merely some obscure regeneration.

Such at least is the meditation of the grown-up buck.

Magnificent knucklehead, this dreamer, grandly flouting his ideas, bears their weight but not without some testiness useful for the brief acts assigned him.

These thoughts, formulated as weapons on his head, for motives of high civility curve backward ornamentally;

Knowing full well, moreover—though of occult source and read-

ily convulsive in his deep sacks—
With what, with what love, he is burdened.

Here then, his phraseology on his head, is what he ruminates between two sallies.

1953-1957

THE EARTH

(Let's just pick up a clod)

This moving mixture of the past of the three kingdoms, all of them spanned, infiltrated, trodden by their seeds and roots, their living avatars: that is earth.

This hash, this forcemeat containing the flesh of the three kingdoms.

Past, not as memory or idea, but as matter.

Matter within anyone's reach, even a baby's; that can be seized by the handful, the shovelful.

If speaking this way of the earth makes me a miner, or earthy, poet, that's just what I want to be! I don't know any greater subject.

While talking about History, someone grabbed a handful of earth and said: "Here's all we know about Universal History. But this we really know, we see, we hold, we have well in hand."

What veneration in these words!

Here too is our aliment; here is where our aliments are prepared. We settle on it as though on History's silos, each clod containing, in seed and root, the future.

For the present, here is our house and garden: the flesh for our houses, the ground for our feet.

And our material for modeling, our toy.

It will always be there for us. We only have to stoop to get some. And it doesn't soil.

It is said that within geosynclines, under enormous pressure, stone is formed anew. Well then, if one is formed, of a particular nature, that is, of earth in the proper sense of the word (improperly called vegetable matter), of those sacred remains, I'd like to see it! No diamond could be more precious!

Here then, is the present image of what we are likely to become. And in this way are the past and the future present.

Everything has gone into it: not only the flesh of the three kingdoms, but the action of the other three elements: fire, air and water.

And space, and time.

What is completely spontaneous in man as he touches the earth is an immediate feeling of familiarity, sympathy, or even veneration, of a filial kind.

Because earth is matter to the highest.

So then, veneration of matter: is anything more fitting for the spirit?

Whereas spirit venerating spirit...can you see that?

—One sees only too much of it.

1944–1949

NOTES ON THE MAKING OF THE PRAIRIE

Translator's Note: I am providing these notes as a way to grant the reader at least a glimpse of this work, which covers four years and sixty-five pages.

Ponge's poetic journal, *La Fabrique du Pré*, records not only the evolution of the poem's anatomy, but more important, the thought process of its creator, which is what fleshes out the poetic skeleton. Starting in August 1960 with the desire to write on the subject— "Ce que j'ai envie d'écrire c'est *Le pré*, un pré entre bois (et rochers) et ruisseau (et rochers)"—Ponge begins a series of reflections on the origin and nature of the prairie.

> A metamorphosis of water and earth, that is, rock reduced to tiny fragments and mixed with all manner of debris from the other kingdoms, vegetable and animal. The whole reduced to infinitesimal grains—and *bedded down*. Which nonetheless stand up and flourish.

Grass is the upright flourishing progeny of these waterbound remains: "a million little breathing pumps that one can press but not repress," laying down its own pipelines, stretching out flat like a printer's plate, a color plate, a reposing color, a bed of color, "and not only the color, but the form invites one to stretch out on it." Crushable but not breakable, the resilient green surface is "a single layer of paint. The underside comes through. Thus it is even more precious than the finest of Persian rugs."

Each image engenders a new thought, a reminiscence: "*A partir d'ici sur ma page, voici le galop. Le galop de l'écriture, selon l'inspiration.*" Moving from one art analogue to another (the color plate, Chagall's *pré*, Persian rugs), Ponge is reminded of Rimbaud's "clavecin des prés" ("Soir historique" in *Les Illuminations)*. The musical analogy seems to him very apt "because in fact the prairie does sound like a harpsichord in contrast to the organ sounds of the nearby forest or continuous melody, the strings of the brook." The thin, short-sounding quality of the harpsichord suggests to him the short-stemmed grasses and flowers of the prairie, a field as varied as the tonal variations of the keyboard.

> A refined, delicate pleasure, though almost prosaic: tedious, less lyric than the organ or the strings (in one of the Bach Brandenburg concertos a very long, varied, insistent, and tedious-in-it-thinness passage of solo harpsichord); on a par with the word, the human voice; rushed or slow, the same rhythm; none of the soaring of the violin, none of the throbbing of the organ, it would seem to come from the mind and the lips, not the heart or the body (the guts)...

Another "galop," from the nature of the thing to the word itself, leads him back to the fifteenth-century composer, Josquin des Prés; the medieval Pré-aux-Clercs and Saint-Germain-des Prés, the former emplacement of the University of Paris, with its evocation of clerics, scholars, disputations, duels, and today, district of antique shops. Going even farther back, Ponge now decides it is time to consult the dictionary. *Pré* is a tract of land for hay or pasture; *Pré-aux-clercs*, a field for scholarly disputation; *sur le pré*, dueling field and moment of decision: *rente de pré*, land revenue—all of which come from the Latin *pratum* (pl. *prata*), whose origin is obscure. "Nothing in all of this of any interest," says Ponge, "not definition, history, or etymology. But Virgil says, 'Sat prata biberunt.' [Ecologue III: "Now then boys, close the sluice gates, the fields have drunk enough."] That is meaningful. Fields saturated with water ...Is it the only word in French from the same family [others listed are prée and préau] ? Certainly not; there is also *prairie*, which is a terrain covered with herbaceous plants for grazing or cutting, hence synonymous with *pré*, which comes from the Vulgar Latin *prataria* for *pratum*."

Since the dictionary yields so little for *pré*, Ponge is inspired to try another tack. Perhaps there is some relationship to be found between the word and its homonyms, *près* (near) and *prêt* (ready).

> Let us look first at *près*. The plural *prés* and the adverb *près* differ only in the direction of the accent (grave or acute), the direction of the bird flying over. *Près*, close in time or space, from the Latin *pressum* (*pressare*: to press, squeeze, push, crowd—doesn't that apply to the grasses of the prairie?). And now *prêt*, ready, prepared for, from the Latin *praestus*. *Praestare* means to furnish (in the sense of allocate). The noun *prêt* is a loan, of money or something else. No attempt is made to explain it. How curious! Nowhere is it related to *paratus*, readied, outfitted.

And yet, it is this origin which Ponge intuits as the reason behind the phonetic proximity of the three words with which "I shall define my pré."

> *Près* (near) both rock and rill, brook, woods and river.
> *Prêt* (ready) for grazing or mowing, ready also to serve as a
>   place for rest or leisurely strolling.
> *Prêt* (loan) from Nature to man and animals...
> Compare also to *prairie*.
> *Pré* is short: freshly cut or mown, never very tall, but upright.
>   And its e has all the value of the diphthongs *ai* and
>   *ie* in *prairie*.

From the etymological possibilities of *pré*, Ponge first extracts its physical qualities, then its associative qualities. It is a place of disputation, decision and brief combat, of death and rebirth. Its own brief dimensions (limited by rocks and hedges), its plants short of stalk, relate to man's dimensions (short of life, short-sounding speech)—"Everything is a question of scale. The prairie is drawn to our scale." It evokes the billiard table (French slang, *le billard*, for operating table), the green baize of the conference table, the field of action for duelists and thinkers, and of repose for vagabonds and dreamers, nymphs and strollers. And finally the word itself, in its own brevity (even its homonyms: drop the s from *près* and the t from *prêt*), is "reduced to the value of a prefix, and even more precisely, the prefix of prefixes, the prefix par excellence, that sounds like a single plucked chord."

The associations are innumerable. Many are discarded, many are repeated, reworked, and eventually appear in the finished poem. But there are numerous fragments that never reappear, such as this one from 1963, except as a shadowed reference.

Ready to give up
stretched out on this prairie
and almost decided to move no more
To remain silent
To die here on top
So as to be placed below
without having to make another move
The sudden awareness
of the verticality of grass
the constant insurrection of green
resuscitates us...
Such is the lyricism of prairies,
the *organism* of prairies
(in the sense that *organism* is the same as *organ*)

[Tr. note: *orgue* in the French, the musical instrument, not *organe*.]

The entries of 1964 mirror the struggle to complete the poem in a back and forth movement that corresponds to the action of memory in conflict with the poet's verbal inspiration.

A rug of rest engendered by a brown page. This rug of rest
and platter of repast was not laid down.
Rather it is the progeny of a page of brown earth...
Suddenly little grains, sands of erudition germinated there.
This rug of rest, of discouragement and resurgence, will
it grow too fast? Let us shear it, mow it as close
as possible.
Let there only be the brown page and grass that in truth
is green.
Let there only be short grass on brown earth; let the
truth today be green.

The problem is to keep the poem as serenely pure as the original experience. But the poetic imagination has a way of galloping off into word plays (like *verité* [truth] and *verte* [green]) and thought associations: "the sands of erudition have germinated."

> No way to get out of it
> Even though this is the place where everything that
> ends begins again...
> No need to get out...of our original onomatopeias.
> Their variety suffices to prove the complexity and
> the truth of life and the world. But they have still
> to be spoken. Said. And perhaps parabolized.
> All of them to be told. To have been told.

He moves forward setting down lines that will stand, then goes back to the early etymological impulse, and even to the memory of the inception of the poem (or essai as he calls it, in the double sense of attempt and genre), noted for the first time in the journal on June 22, 1964—a day after the lines quoted above were entered. Walking through a pine grove with his wife, "was it a Sunday?" in 1960, he perceived a prairie stretching alongside a little river with groups of strollers on it. "That was all. Nothing more...I was, I don't know why, taken with a kind of enthusiasm, secret, calm, pure, tranquil. I knew immediately that this vision would remain as it was, intact in my memory. And that I had to try and tell it. To understand it? Understand is not the word. To try and hold on to its promised delight and to penetrate it, communicate it. Why?"

The answer is clear in an entry that dates from the final month of the journal, July 1964.

> The prairie, then, is hope, resurrection, in its most elemen-
> tal, unique, ingenuous sense, but stretched horizontally
> before our eyes for our relaxation, our repose. It is the field
> of our rest prepared (*préparé*)—past participle comprising all
> elements, all past action, and memory, the remembrance of
> the totality of past actions. Totality, the field into which have
> entered the remains of the three kingdoms. Accumulation of
> past days and principle of today's day.

THE PRAIRIE

When Nature, at our awaking, sometimes proposes to us
Precisely what we were intending,
Praise at once swells in our throats.
We think we are in paradise.

So it was with the prairie I wish to tell of,
And which provides my subject for today.

Since this has more to do with a way of being
Than with a platter set before our eyes,
The word is more fitting than paint
Which would not do at all.

Taking a tube of green and spreading it on the page
Does not make a prairie.
They are born in another way.
They surge up from the page.
And the page should furthermore be brown.

Let us then prepare the page on which today may be born
A verdant verity.

Sometimes then—we might also say in some places—
Sometimes, our nature
I mean by that Nature on our planet
And what we are each day on awaking—
Sometimes, our nature has prepared us (for) a prairie.

But what is it that blocks our way?
In this little underbrush half-shade half-sun,
Who sets these spokes in our wheels?

Why, as soon as we emerge over the page,
In this single paragraph, so many scruples?

Why then, seen from here, this limited fragment of space,
Stretched between four rocks or four hawthorn hedges,
Barely larger than a handkerchief,
Moraine of the forests, downpour of adverse signs,
This prairie, gentle surface, halo of springs and of the original
storm sweet sequel
In unanimous anonymous call or reply to the rain,
Why does it suddenly seem more precious to us
Than the finest of Persian rugs?

Fragile but not frangible,
The soil at times reconquers the surface
Marked by the little hooves of the foal that galloped
there,
Trampled by the cattle that pushed slowly toward the
watering place...
While a long procession of Sunday strollers, without
Soiling their white shoes, moves ahead
Following the little stream, swollen by drowning or
perdition,
Why then, from the start, does it prohibit us?

Could we then already have reached the naos,
That sacred place for a repast of reasons?
Here we are, in any case, at the heart of pleonasms
And at the only logical level that befits us.
Here the prayer wheel is already turning,
Yet without the slightest idea of prostration,
For that would be contrary to the verticalities of the place.

Crasis of *paratus*, according to Latin etymologists,
Close [*près*] to rock and rill, Ready [*prêt*] to be mown or grazed,

Prepared for us by nature,
Pré, paré, près, prêt.

The prairie [pré] lying there like the ideal past participle
Is equally revere(d) end as our prefix of prefixes,
Pre-fix within prefix, pre-sent within present.

No way out of our original onomatopeias.
In that case, back into them.

No need, furthermore, to get out,
Their variations being adequate to account

For the marvelously tedious Monotony and Variety of the world.
For its perpetuity, in short.

Yet must they be pronounced.
Spoken. And perhaps parabolized.
All of them, told.

....

(Here a long passage should intervene somewhat like the interminable harpsichord solo of the Fifth Brandenburg Concerto, that is, tedious and mechanical, yet at the same time mechanizing, not so much because of the music as the logic, reasoning from the lips, not the chest or the heart—in which I shall try to explain, and I mean explain, two or three things: to begin with, if pré, in French, represents one of the most important and primordial of logical notions, it holds equally true for the physical (geophysical), since what is involved is a metamorphosis of water which, instead of evaporating, at the summons of heat, directly into clouds, chooses here by clinging to the earth and passing through it, that is, through the kneaded remains of the past of the three kingdoms and particularly through the finest granulations of the mineral kingdom, ultimately reimpregnating the universal ashtray—to renew life in its most elementary form, grass: element-aliment. This chapter, which is *also* to be the music of the prairies, will sound thin and elaborate, with numerous appoggiaturas, so as to end (if it ends) both accelerando and rinforzando, in a kind of thunderclap which makes us seek refuge in the woods. The perfecting of this passage could easily take me a few more years. However it turns out...)

....

The original storm spoke at length.

....

Did the original storm not thunder so long within us precisely so that

       —for it rolls away, only
       partially filling the lower
       horizon where it lightens still—
Readying for the most urgent, rushing to the most pressing,
We would leave these woods,
Would pass between these trees and our remaining scruples,
And, leaving behind all portals and colonnades,
Transported suddenly by a quiet enthusiasm
For a verity that might today be verdant,
Would soon find ourselves stretched out on this prairie,
Long ago prepared for us by nature
          —where nothing matters any
          more but the blue sky.
The bird flying over it in the opposite direction to writing
Reminds us of the concrete; and its contradiction,
Marking the differential note of *pré*,
Whether *près* or *prêt*, or the *prai* of prairie,
Sounds short and sharp like the tearing
Of meaning in the all too clear sky.

For the place of long discussion can just as well
Become the place of decision.

Of two equals standing on arrival, one at least,
After a crossed assault with oblique weapons,

Will remain lying, First above, then below.

Here then, on this prairie, is the occasion, as befits,
To come to an end, prematurely.

Gentlemen typesetters,
Place here, I beg you, the final dot.

Then, beneath, with no spacing added, lay my name,
In lower case, naturally,
      Except the initials, of course,
      Since they are also the initials
      Of Fennel and Parsnip which
      Tomorrow will be growing up on top.

      Francis Ponge

O THIS IS WHY I HAVE LIVED

Les Fleurys, night of 19–20 July 1961

Taking an intense pleasure in doing nothing
but provoking (by my mere presence
charged with a kind of magnetism
for the being of things; this presence being
in some way exemplary: through the intensity
of its tranquillity (smiling, indulgent),
through the power of its patience,
the power of the example of its existence
accomplished in tranquillity, in repose,
through the power of the example of its health)
but provoking an intensification
of the true, authentic, unadorned nature
of beings and things;
nothing but awaiting it, awaiting that very moment

Doing nothing but awaiting
their particular declaration
And then fixing it, immobilizing it, petrifying it
   (Sartre calls it) for eternity, fulfilling it
or better yet helping it (without me it would not be
possible) to fulfill itself.

Doing nothing but writing slowly black on white
—very slowly, attentively, very black on very white.

I stretched out
alongside beings and things
Pen in hand, my writing table
(a blank page) on my knees.

I have written, it has been published, I have lived.
I have written, they have lived, I have lived.

Jean Follain
1893-1971

Introduction by Mary Feeney

Canisy
Translated by Louise Guiney

A World Rich in Anniversaries
Translated by Mary Feeney
and William Matthews

Jean Follain was born to a middle-class family in Canisy, a small Normandy town just south of St. Lô. He has chronicled this rich provincial world, anchored in the 19th century, in his prose works *Canisy* and *Chef-Lieu*—a world figuratively shattered by what the French call the War of 1914, then literally by World War II. Follain's writing, while devoid of nostalgia, is marked by an effort to recreate the past. In his quest for the paradoxical "eternal moment," he studded his poetry with references to history, ritual, uniforms, and long-forgotten household objects. Each of his densely worked prose pieces is less a vignette, or even a poem, than a smal world in itself.

Follain studied law at Caen, leaving Normandy in 1925 for further studies and a clerkship in Paris. As a child, one of his favorite pastimes had been studying the map of Paris and memorizing the capital's street names. The city did not disappoint. He soon became part of the Sagesse group of writers, publishing his first poems in the review of the same name in 1928. He came to know many more writers, including Max Jacob, and published widely, eventually settling with the famed house of Gallimard, where all the volumes cited in this introduction appeared. In 1934, he married Madeleine Denis, daughter of the Nabi artist Maurice Denis, herself a painter under the name Madeleine Dinès.

As his literary and artistic circles widened, Follain also advanced in his legal career, eventually becoming a judge in 1951. He retired from the judiciary in 1959, traveling extensively as well as increasing his literary output.

On a long walk home from an evening literary gathering in Paris on March 10, 1971, Jean Follain was struck and killed by a car exiting a traffic tunnel near the Place de la Concorde.

William Matthews and I had begun translating Follain's prose poems in the spring of 1970. The texts are found in two collections, *Tout Instant* (1957) and *Appareil de la Terre* (1964). Bill and I divided the poems in half, each producing a set of rough drafts, which we revised during periodic work sessions over the next year and a half. For the 1971-72 academic year, I was a teaching assistant at a suburban Paris high school. I contacted Follain's widow, Madeleine, who generously reworked the poems with me from January to June 1972. In the process, we became fast friends.

Bill and I then again revisited the texts, culling a book, which we titled *A World Rich in Anniversaries*, from our ninety-three original translations. Grilled Flowers Press published the first edition in 1979 with a 1981 reissue under the name Logbridge-Rhodes. Shortly before his untimely death in 1997, Bill began working with White Pine Press to reissue the translations.

The texts translated by Louise Guiney, with the assistance of Madeline Follain, are from *Canisy*, also published by Logbridge-Rhodes in 1981. Guiney, a freelance translator based in Paris, was introduced to Follain's work and his widow, Madeleine, by Mortimer Guiney, at the time a member of the University of Connecticut Department of Romance and Classical Languages. This contact with Madeleine Follain also developed into an enduring and richly productive friendship. Madeleine's conribution to the vitality of her husband's literary legacy cannot be overestimated. Her patient guidance and encouragement of translators, scholars, and publishers following her husband's death were crucial in bringing his work to a larger public.

> "There was a door. The top part had four panes of glass in it, covered with blue glazing paper and separated by a piece of wood in the shape of a cross. the blue stood for toil and forbearance. Rich or poor, despite finicky hatreds, they were the kin who liked dedicating their daughters to blue."

It is with these words that Follain opens the door to his childhood and invites us in. More than that, though, he has, in just four sentences, painted for us a picture of the entire world of the childhood we are about to encounter. He begins with the simple fact of a door, he then brings in the main religious image of his culture, values of his village. In what seems unusual for a reminiscence about childhood, the boy's parents are barely mentioned. What he has tried to record and create is the world that, as he stated, vanished with the war of 1914–1918. Clearly, memory is of supreme importance to Follain, an "analogue for the imagination," as the poet and novelist Robert Morgan said in his 1979 essay "Insect, Bowl, Horizon," discussing the original Grilled Flowers edition of *A World Rich in Anniversaries*.

"If you were commanded to forget certain things," Follain wrote, "it would be better to be found like that man who went mad as a result of the conscription under the empire, among the moles and lizards around a dismantled belfry." But to Follain, it is not mere remembrance of what no longer exists that makes memory so important. Rather, memory is the key that unlocks mysteries of the present. Follain has, by recording the details of his childhood, shown us a rite of passage that invokes an endless procession of passages stretching both back and forward while maintaining a sense of the unchanging that allows us to "rediscover a certain innocence of the world which is not illusion but profound truth, and which subsists...in the face of everything, and despite all of history's diabolical tricks."

Follain involves us in the discovery of community, of things, animals, people, emotions, and even the community of time. Binding these communities together is language. As Follain discovered when he was sent to England in 1919 to learn English, the words he had learned to name things were part of the uniqueness of the things named. To give something another name was merely to create analogy, a comparison of sorts.

"There is much thickness and distance in these little texts," Robert Morgan wrote of the prose poems. "The most casual seems to reach so far and so fast back toward space we are tempted to call it surrealism. But the real power in Follain is clearly the accuracy in the unexpected conjugations. The strangeness derives from the freshness of seeing."

Follain revealed his *ars poetica* in a 1967 speech: "The poem can find its genesis in an everyday figure of speech, suddenly perceived glutted with all its meaning, surrounded by a kind of magnetic aura. A simple object, never before seen in such a way and charged with its full meaning, can also trigger the poem...Much is said about the use of images in poetry. It is certain that in the broad sense of the term, all poetry contains images. In the narrower sense, many poems contain similes and metaphors. Numerous poets today and in the past have given us admirable examples. As far as I am concerned, I have come to the point of writing almost none at all. Perhaps because simile and metaphor imply comparison, and I can compare no one thing to any other in this multifarious universe nonetheless full of mysterious affinities between all things. I have sometimes felt, charmed by other poets' metaphors and similes, that I wanted to write my own, did and found them satisfactory, then disowned them all the next day upon realizing they are simply not me...There are curious connnections between the poet's art and that of the painter. I may say to myself, looking at a text: I need some red there, or some gray or other; but of course I don't get my red by putting some red thing in my text, but, for example, by adding a pronoun or some syllable of a word which, for me, is a stroke of red...As Mallarmé said to Degas, poetry is not made of ideas, but of words; in any case, poetry is made, he stated, to 'Give the tribe's words back their full and the purest meaning, their true weight and all their freshness.' Meaning the poet must, unless consciously rejuvenating one, disdain clichés, evidence that a vocable is wearing out. 'You settle for little or nothing,' said Francis Ponge, 'if to express grandeur you simply use the word grandeur.' As for myself, I would rather see muted brilliance than too much brilliance in poetry. Jean Cocteau expressed the same thing by saying he liked the wrong side of certain bright colored silk ties, full of attenuated brilliance and subtle iridescence, better than the right side of the same ties...What is essential in poetry is an absence of vagueness as well as of stiffness in writing...It appears that poetry eminently linked to the beauty of the universe is assured of perennial existence. Poetry tries desperately to free this beauty and all the ineffable, even the tragic, it keeps in the context of the world..."

As his centenary approaches, Follain's work remains magnetic. Interest in his writing grows in France, where a three-day Follain conference was held in March 2002 at the University of Besançon. I know William Matthews joined me in the hope that this new edition will attract further readers to this timeless work.

—Mary Feeney

from CANISY

There was a door. The top part had four panes of glass in it, covered with blue glazing paper and separated by a piece of wood in the shape of a cross. The blue stood for toil and forbearance. Rich or poor, despite finicky hatreds, they were the kind who liked dedicating their daughters to blue.

This door was replaced by a solid one painted to look like oak and I watched the scales of several summers cover it over until finally it was painted one color. Its big brass doorknob was polished now and then by women who were not quite able to repress the tears of their rustic pain.

The old door opened once, and the new one opens still, into my maternal grandmother Heussebrot's house, in Canisy, where I was born.

The photograph of my grandfather Heussebrot, the country lawyer, showing him amid a group of men who are still young, survives. They are all dressed in suits neither cut nor style of which will ever return just as they were during those years on the earth.

The family kept his dictionary. On the front page the schoolboy wrote: "This dictionary belongs to Jean Heussebrot as France belongs to the king."

He often, for auctions that were far away, would set out in a horse-drawn carriage, not returning until nightfall. One night, as he passed Bishop's Pond, he heard what seemed to be a whistled signal and, though gentle with the horses as a rule, he whipped his mare, and with her quickened pace raised from the darkened ground a rosary of sparks.

Ever since first hearing that story, carriage rushing towards safety, sinister whistling all around it, sky above as dark as ink, the vision of ponds has roused in me an aura of tapestry, and of farewells.

The snuff-box belonging to my paternal grandfather, the school-master, closed with a dry click, disturbing for a moment, as we walked past, the calm of cornstalk and buttercup.

One day the infantry camped in town. How gravely did I con-template, to the very trembling of the fringe on their epaulettes, these soldiers, these inspirers of dreams in which passion, religion and pre-eminences intermingled.

Room was made around the table with the fawn-colored oil cloth for those whose billeting ticket sent them to the school. Here and there a reflected flame burnished a cuirass or turned red and saturnine the faded madder of a trouser-leg. They drank virgin cider resplendent as a golden lacquer, and the schoolmaster kept them company.

A very distant image is one of old mother Simon, mother to Florentine, my maternal grandmother's servant. On her I bestowed the quasi-Asiatic name of mother Yon-Yon. White cotton cap on her head, dressed in rough gray clothes, she always, when entering the mosaic vestibule, took care not to make any noise with her wooden shoes.

Her grave was still fresh when I saw it, not a single blade of grass had yet sprung up between the clods of earth. She was born in 1830, a time, in villages without machines, when noise rang clear and when the sorcerer lived in a house whose mud baked in the sun while he kept watch from his doorstep, clothed in the flow-ered waistcoat of a lord.

I was five years old when my brother was born. The texture of that day's bread is with me now, and the warm brown of the stew lying in a round dish with its amber-colored potatoes. Florentine the servant and my maternal grandmother kept their ears open while they ate to catch the slightest sound. And when I first heard the newborn infant cry, I vaguely sensed, through the hot dishes' steam, and beyond confusing tales of babies bought at fairs or found under cabbages, that the world is world, and children are born into it, human offspring come from the dark, molded by the will of fragile mothers.

Replete with parish affairs, set on a rustic, Christian course, Florentine the servant, when told of a paternal passion considered exaggerated in some quarters once said: "What can you expect? It's his own."

She used to carry me in her arms and let me scribble on the immaculate peak of her white cap with the lead from an old pencil.

She sang me the song about little Paul, a song trembling with all the idealized tears of field and slum:

> When Paul was scarcely five years old
> His mother up to Heaven rose.
> So as not to make him cry and weep
> They told him she was fast asleep.

It was from the church pew of Florentine's sister Mary that I sometimes witnessed the choral Vesper services on Sundays. The men in the choir wore copes embroidered with red roses; in cassock and surplice, gathered with them around the music stand, were the players: double bass, cornet, trombone.

Hidden in my tall pew, enclosed on every side as though in a little house, I turned my back to the altar and sat down on the small bench provided for kneeling. I thus had, before me, like a table, a part of the big, varnished wooden seat and I took biscuits shaped like tiny little men and women and spread them out on it, arranging and examining each one with care before eating it, gnawing, here and there, on a head or a pair of legs. Meanwhile the voices of the choir, which always lingered over the neumes, began to gather speed, swelling the verses of the psalms with all sorts of little embellishments unknown to Gregorian chant. Inside my pew I was surrounded by the warm and ample dresses of country women whose housewifely thoughts merged with the invocations to the Virgin surging upwards from the sumptuous stanzas of the *Magnificat* and dissolving in a cloud of incense inhaled by my nostrils, as my lace collar wilted a little in the miasmas of the bronze dusk, and in my mouth I hoarded, in a ball, my chewed-up little men, elastic dough, sweet sugared clay.

...

The woodbin in my maternal grandmother's big kitchen was the first piece of furniture I ever took a liking to. It stood between the vast hearth and a corner of the room, imprisoning the corner behind its two molded oaken panels.

Whenever it was not completely filled with logs and kindling, I'd climb inside, make believe it was a church pulpit, and launch into sermons which, however, never got further than the exordium, for I was short on conclusions and primarily interested in pronouncing the unaccustomed words: dearly beloved brethren. Also from the woodbin, now a lecture platform at the Sorbonne, I'd embark on interminable discourses taken word for word straight from the very books that made the least sense to me, old treatises on philosophy and theology bursting with strange vocables whose magic I longed to divine and whose rambling phrases wove a complicated filigree into the fabric of everyday life. Amid faggot and firewood thus I reigned when I was seven years old. I was now and then dislodged by a fresh provision of logs my maternal grandmother brought back from the shed outside in her black apron with the little white flowers on it. But if she was only bringing up charcoal from the cellar in a faded, dented toy pail, then I'd stay in my woodbin, while she fed the charcoal to the small white enameled brick stove with the blue stars on it and stirred her sauces with a steady hand, as night came on and her face, glinting with two tiny golden earrings, began to blur.

There were sparrows and fruits carved across the front of the big cupboard with gleaming locks and hinges. On its double doors would often be reflected a flame from the huge fireplace, a cavern filled with shrouds of soot and ringing with the minor-key song of rising steam. Sitting beside the fire in his stiff smock, left to himself on a chilly Sunday morning would be a hired hand while upstairs, to the sound of muffled footsteps and tumbling eiderdowns and pillows, bedrooms were being turned out. He'd be waiting for the midday meal because on Sundays it was customary to invite for dinner anyone who had worked for the household towards the end of the week. The man would have gone to early, low Mass and then on to the house where he was to be a guest. With time to kill before dinner he'd sit down, read the paper perhaps: *Le Courrier*, mostly filled with auction notices, or else he'd just sit there, his hands on his knees. Brought a jug of cider and a tumbler, he'd pour a glass, wait a minute then throw his head back and drink down the red liquid in one gulp; four or five minutes later he'd pour himself another and drink it down the same way, in the shrouded Sunday morning silence.

...

The shed where the casks were kept had walls of clay. I tore pieces of it off, wet them, shaped them into little statues; then, bored, dissatisfied, I destroyed them. And when the wind knocks a piece of broken slate from the roof, what can you do with the flakes from it? Crush them to a powder. I had already produced red powder by banging a piece of brick with a hammer. I liked to crush pebbles down fine for making stone flour—lavender, pink, yellow—I ground it up, put it in bags and made believe it was some rare and magical concoction. Walking in the mud, seeing the pattern the soles of my shoes made as they sank down was a joy to me, there's no denying it; and the fleeting imprint of hobnailed boots in dust awakened in me even more, perhaps, a disturbing apprehension of the universe. Distracted, I ran into the swing hanging from the branches of the apple tree whose placid fruit was slowly changing color. You could do anything you liked with this fruit; carve meridians around it, sculpt a baroque face onto it, cut slices out of it and then throw them away. With a pair of scissors you could make cut-outs in the leaves, changing patterns, altering outlines. The geranium flower gave a juice like blood; what was to stop you from smearing your face with it like a clown, object of my sinuous dreams?

...

My maternal grandmother, the lawyer's widow, was very fond of my grandfather the schoolmaster. She called him "the father," he called her "madame." She'd take him with her to visit her farms, especially when she went on foot to the one at Mesnil Amey.

They'd be a good hour on the main highway. For part of the way, this main highway was red, then, its geological context changing, it turned blue-black. In between these two zones was an intermediate, violet-colored, one. Hedgerows lined the way and there was nothing to distract the eye except one hamlet and the open throat of a cold forge.

Holding his horn-handled cane, my grandfather always started out briskly like a pioneer, but he tired quickly and before long he'd be mopping his brow with his poppy-red handkerchief, its polka dots black as their hearts. "I can't go on, madame," he'd say. "We're almost there, the father," she'd reply and, thus reassured, he'd again put on a little speed.

Soon catching sight of a pile of pebbles, however, he'd announce: "I can't go any farther, madame, I will wait for you here," and with that, down he would sit on the stones. My grandmother, imperturbable, knowing perfectly well what would happen next, didn't even slow down.

Seeing my grandmother's slender form grow smaller, the father would rise from his seat of rock, Cronstadt hat so black upon his head under the vibrant azure, fleetingly caress his small white beard and hasten after her, crying, "Madame, madame wait for me," and she waited for him, smiling and serene.

...

The mighty edifices of nightfall: triumphal arches formed by foliage at the end of avenues, labyrinths of cool paths, fields like coliseums with hedgerows for bleachers all the way to the horizon, porticos and dolmens of cloud framing our childhood being as it travelled towards its destiny.

The thunderstorm opened numberless perspectives and through the windowpanes I watched people who with bent heads braved it and thought they too labored for my well-being. I never did see a tree flying through the air during the storm, or an entire thatched roof, as sometimes happened.

Thunder and lightning frightened me. At every lightning flash I made the sign of the cross as my grandmothers did. We sat around the table waiting for the storm to end. The moment they saw the sky cloud over the huge sheets drying in the stiffling hot gardens were brought inside.

There were also days of raging sun, solitary postmen on the roads.

Men cut grain and flower at a single stroke.

Behind the hedge appears a hated neighbor's face. He feels as hot as they do, maybe more so, they see it and rejoice without digging deeper into their souls.

A bell toll in this burning afternoon meanwhile reminded us we were in Christendom. Summer torpor stilled yellowing tufts of grass at isolated crossroads, grass resistant to uprooting and that, in any case, no one ever thought of uprooting. For an instant the sound of a pump in a courtyard. Ah, constant glory of the sun at the foot of calvaries, constant color of Christianity and force of necessity, the piece of history we were part of, children in our black school smocks!

In gardens curving around flower beds sat people lost in thought, women with their proverbs and blacksmiths their halo, didn't they all, good or bad, use the same word for designating that common flower the rose? A rose they would say, and if they didn't say it they thought it, and the flower left its mark in them.

That was the time when the wall with the spider webs where the frail plants grew waited for someone to lean against it, and the coming of night delivered the heat from the stone.

In front of the big fireplace you could pretend history's convolutions might someday bring an extraordinary personage to sit down there: emperor or king, a leader of peoples who in the fire-light would assume the ordinary figure of a man, soften his glance and even, perhaps, being very tired, completely close his eyes.

A World Rich in Anniversaries

Opening his hands, a man thinks; Meticulous bakers, it is with you we live when reading wearies us. You can't keep insects from lying trapped in the bread dough. Giving a huge loaf to a child who will take it back to his village over a couple of miles away, you say: Can you carry it all the way, it's heavy, can you make it? Women, seeing the tears of dough on an apprentice's forearm, feel a vague tenderness at the same time the sun blazes on their thatched cottages. The big round loaves in woven baskets show crevices and burnt spots, and, when cut, those smooth-walled holes known as their eyes.

A boy is troubled on a day petals pour down and dogs are stolid. Girls get straight up out of bed, sun falls on their torsos, a wasp buzzes in the fold of a curtain; the calendar on the wall grows warm. Men are drinking in the blind alley where some feeble plants poke up. A conference searches for peace without finding it. In a bedroom, a turn-of-the-century breastplate gleams, well polished. When French regiments wore ones like it, Maurice Maindron wrote cloak-and-dagger novels; he loved armor, a love inspired by his taste for coleoptera. Now a May beetle the color of dead leaves proceeds across the glittering breastplate at this moment—possible as all things are possible—this moment which will never return.

The landscapes they walk through unseeing measure their lives; they tell themselves night should come pretty early. They look for an inn on a former battlefield. Once the plumes of a captain's headgear concealed an impassive insect while the scarlet-coated captain felt fear approach. On his aging mount, he would master it. Spikey grasses, lobed leaves, ivy corymbs waver in a daydream of women's faces. In the hamlet the color of burnt bread, one woman, far from death and tilting back her head, lets her milk-swollen breast be kissed in the cool half-light.

The cress-peddler, hardly a customer richer, disappears along the distance of the plain, as if to meet the coppered color of an old horizon. He never stops pondering the way shoes wear out. At the same time, in the village, several men meet at one of their mother's house. She tells them, displaying her dead husband's pistols: Guns are the jewelry of men. She also declares she does not hate those gypsy girls who, despite their gaudy clothes, hip-swinging and smiles, sometimes maintain a deep reserve. When night comes down on the hedgerows without seeming to be a curse, you can hear drum practice reverberating in the courtyard of the rectory, now headquarters.

As in the city theater curtains rise, in the country the able-bodied men and the disabled ones—clearer-eyed, much stronger in the arms—go night-walking at the edge of a meadow. Then they have to strain to catch, far off, the yipping of wire-haired dogs with worn-down collars. One of them can't hear the dullest and most distant barking. When they've spent enough time treading down the dark grass, stones around them and huge trees, they go back to the house with smooth benches where the fire will be banked with ashes until dawn, and the clock will not stop scanning the minutes of a history forever improvising.

There's no more war. The ocean is distant. The wide river flowing through the city reflects domes and archways. Some people are already asleep on makeshift beds of rags and papers. It's the first day of winter. Motor cars drive through the swiftly fallen night. There are almost no more horses. Still, the clatter of horseshoes is a sound familiar enough not to surprise you. Nor does the jingle of bells on a collar, the masterwork of a harness-maker always up at the crack of dawn, in command of himself and yet subject to the anguishes of night.

On Easter Sunday the old man puts jewelry onto the wrists, ears, and neck of a long-haired woman. Already hitched to the black and yellow carriage, the glistening bay mare whinnies. A sailor sings by an engraving of the end of the world with Christ in the billowy heavens, the dead caught in their shrouds, leaving their graves. Time fills up with a future that may be fearsome. A child goes by on the road, wearing a motionless garter snake for a bracelet. How hot this long day beginning a century will be! Housebound, a deformed girl closes her blue eyes.

To know how a leaf feels, look into it for the earth ready to quake in perhaps ten thousand years. For now, the leaf-stalk holds out, tight to the branch. Colors change with the different times of day. In the distance a man shouts, hands around his mouth to carry his voice. He has years to live yet, but he has never seen the sea, nor will he. In two whole centuries none of his ancestors saw it, except one, dead in the revolution, falsely accused of treason, who always used to wash his hands at the stroke of noon in the old greened-over fountain.

One day I suddenly notice this object within my sight for ten years and which in fact I had never truly seen. Likewise men forget the knick-knacks in their bedrooms, the patterns of their wallpaper, the faces on their andirons, until the day death takes them, as the saying goes, without formalities. Suddenly this forgotten bowl speaks to me, imposes its presence. I'm afraid it will fall from my hands, and on the rug depicting two elephants and their howdahs nothing will be left of it but shining fragments that have to be picked up sadly. The bowl was once washed by chattering maidservants surrounded by clouds and vapors, framed in glints of copper and tin. The world was new. In those days many men killed. Now everything plots without them against nothingness, even in the capitals where torture chambers have come back again. I think it over, the bowl in my hands. Whatever craftsman fashioned it perhaps kept a proud look about him, a modest glance, was perhaps alone in the world.

A chant goes up from every object. The craftsman enclosed in it a bit of his body that had known love well, then carried a long illness, or simply succumbed to old age. Chant of wood, steel, copper. Across the centuries you hear henchmen snicker, girls laugh with wild voices, madwomen bleat, a baby gurgle. But the object doesn't vanish. You find such multifarious things in travelers' pockets: penknives, small notebooks, a minuscule screw left over from some dismantling, a tangled piece of string, a few carrot or parsnip seeds—the same kind of seeds the man, bent toward the earth, threw in the little furrow he'd dug in the fenced yard's flowerbed, back when he was a homebody. The horizon thins out before the eyes of a man out taking a walk. His mind carries many a secret, scraps of love, desires that are one moment solid but then evaporate, while the object, even if he's forgotten it, stays in his pocket like a talisman. Rummaging through the old clothes your thickening body no longer fits—the body death keeps an eye on, even if at a distance—you find the movement of a frail machine. You have to think hard to remember what it's for. You turn it over and over in your fingers while a legendary sun sets, far away.

The fineness of things gives the universe nobility. Behind each thing a password lies hidden. These fragile cups, these crystal glasses, how carefully they must be put in the cupboard! The maid gets up on a chair when they belong on the highest shelf. They link us to the world whose tarnished images blur together. In the same way a boy, seeing old straw beehives, thinks of the Gauls' huts in his *History of France*. Suppose the boy's mother happens to say to him, "You're heartless," and the sentence echoes deeper and deeper inside him. The world around him is veiled, sadness hangs heavily on roofs with weathervanes depicting a variety of things, even racehorses ridden by their jockeys. Sadness covers everything, even toys. It's sadness for the end of the world, for the last judgment. "No," the child answers, "I'm not a bad boy, because I cried when grandfather died." "Maybe so," the mother comes back, "but you aren't always good." That's like telling him he's good sometimes, anyway. So the universe clears up again, things regain their glitter, clouds are proud and graceful. Once more, decorations and everyday things sparkle. You hear the saw grinding into wood, food boiling, even if it's one of those monotonous long days that persist in having been, long after the memory of them is gone.

She stops short at something said to her, holding at arm's length the plate she'd just put on the table. Outside, the air's pure, it seems nothing should be a secret. When the children shout too loud, she says to them, "Listen, I can't hear a thing." The children play all sorts of games under the table; they're soldiers, generals, priests, then they become schoolteachers. Above them the table is being set. The dishes don't match anymore: one's all white, another has the branch of an indeterminate tree on it and on top of that a bird, pink as the branch. A third plate is hexagonal, one of its points chipped off. A fourth is rimmed in gold. Glasses have also been set. The forks are tin. The knives have black handles. A little girl comes out of the next room, the one she wasn't supposed to go into. Walking along, she holds an outsized geography book open in front of her and reads, stressing each syllable: "The earth is round like a ball." On the table now there are salt crystals and, on a large platter, the food in its sauce that looks like black lacquer.

Close attention to things may make them seem strange. Removed from time as they are, won't they grow frozen in eternity? Things no longer in use—or whose proper use has been forgotten—are bewildered: carved flint hatchets abandoned in a showcase, museum ewers, the sarcophagus a peasant has turned into a pig trough. A horseshoe might also be found along the road one wartime morning. As for the tramp carrying a battered canteen and odd bits of scrap metal, his knowing eye examines each find he plucks from the footpath, the hedgerow, or even the heap of dirt abuzz with the summer's flies.

Should the schoolboy pull a marble out of his pocket, the soldier an old familiar knife, the schoolmaster a huge colored handkerchief, it might be that for a brief instant, such objects, humble as they are, seem priceless. A whole world rich in anniversaries is revealed when a matron takes out from beneath stacks of linen in a large closet, a baptismal box containing First Communion pictures with their golden chalices and red and blue Savior. In a spare moment she opens this precious box only to close it after a short, silent contemplation, since of course the clock is always striking: time to sweep, time to sew, time too for feeding the animals that complain when they get no fodder, mash, or bloody scraps.

There are moments the child isn't drawn to his toys, whether old or brand new. He feels the silence surrounding objects in the house, which keeps it special smell in spite of everything. Quite differently from toys the elements will attract him, above all fire and water. It's a turbid joy he'll feel watching a cardboard horse burn. Likewise he'll be able to change dry earth to mud he'll handle for hours, eager for mystery. There's also, for his delight, sumptuous matter: the soot from tall chimneys forms thick shells, forms crusts, and falls off in slabs. Didn't this soot, pulverized and mixed with wine, once serve as ink for village scriveners? As night comes on, the child's curiosity subsides. While sometimes a drunk, singing to keep his hopes up, pack slung over his shoulder, starts on his floundering but irreversible path into the silent traitor of a pond, where he dies.

The women washing dishes were full of talk. You could hear glasses and bowls colliding. Through calm windows you could see a large shed containing several wheels, one from a tricycle, another from a child's stroller pushed so long, so ceremoniously beneath the sycamores. Sometimes the women would stop; still holding porcelain plates in their hands, they'd tilt their heads, squinting a little, trying to remember a forgotten name or date. At their feet, the cat licked milk from a saucer. The future was nonetheless full of hideous landscapes, bloody barracks bitten by the sand, stupor in armored railroad cars. For the time being, it was unheard of. There was the neatness of table settings and shining kitchen utensils touching the softened skin of the dishwashers, these women who, in a couple of hours, would say: "It's getting dark, let's light the lamps, you can't see a thing."

Some territories are neither completely country nor completely city. Plants are coated with dust as they grow. Laundry dries in small fenced-in lots. People from these places have the look of exiles. Still they can be seen rocking babies, bringing home from small, shabby stores their groceries, packaged food, boxes with pictures of factories in linear perspective. Putting the packages on the table, they say: "I didn't meet a soul." Their son looks at them; he's holding a puppet with peeling paint that he'll soon give up, and then he'll only look for pebbles along the road. Old as they are, they become his favorite toys.

Hamlets still keep the smell they had in frugal times, back when fieldhands rarely ate meat. In blinding light near a pile of old stones with valerian growing among them, near a broken-down fence, is where the subtle smell of poor country rises to the sky. If dogs bark as they did in Gaul, or Palestine in the days of Christ, it's because they hear a cart full of country youth in modern dress. When the team of sturdy horses appears, the vapor of time gone by scatters with the cries of sunstruck boys and girls: the landscape comes together again at this summons to the present, agrees to it.

This plant, so exceptional since its flower never lasts more than a few hours, broke into blossom on a morning the garden's owners weren't at home. With its speckled petals, it bends in the breeze like so many other more common flowers. There's a terrible sweetness to everything. A colony of armored insects, old gold, has moved into a shaded corner. Nearby, people hurry up and down steps. A hand stops on the rail of an oaken stairway; every minute falls. At six in the evening, the flower will be withered, the horizon will begin to grow pale, a group of girls will start to sing with no weakness or shame.

You can get the impression that cities are really our point of contact with fate, spreading out their shimmering perspectives, the fans of their back streets. Hallways end at brown doors: behind them, you hardly hear the muffled sounds of couples. People don't always pass each other with blank faces. Sometimes their glances seem vulnerable. Often the public clocks are stopped: then time goes nowhere. But dawn, with its tranquil beauty, will bathe some monument's steeple or dome, or the first flowers in an indoor market where a freshly washed woman cries Roses for Sale.

The county groundskeeper picks wilted flowers and puts them in little piles. If you looked through the basement window, you could see the baker painting his brioches with beaten eggs. On a high rung of an extension ladder, a signpainter meticulously begins a capital letter beneath the sky this burning month has driven to distraction.

A fountain topped by a grotesque grimacing mask no longer works. "What can you do?" says a voice behind shutters. Between cobblestones, a plant has pushed out a yellow shoot that just might end up not being crushed by someone. Minuscule plants growing in the cracks of walls have the best chance of survival. Lead gutters show their blue-gray. In a courtyard hammering speaks of slow, steady work. Finally, the wind comes down from the hill where tombs stand.

Store windows start to light up: displays that banish thoughts of war or hunger, huge dolls with lifelike lashes, eyelids that close. A storefront with shining jewels catches your eye. A white wall takes on a greengage tint. A gutter along the sidewalk seems to be running with a red liqueur instead of dirty water. Absinthe-green smoke floats up from mute roofs. There's a passerby who's never written a word except his signature, using a pen with a beat-up wooden holder. He senses this bursting beauty. And the man with a terrible temper, seeing his hand turned orange by the sunset, stops short, falls silent before his household who fear him, maybe even forgive him his fits.

A crossroads, said to be treacherous. But quiet. A man was seen there whittling green wood into a whistle for a boy in an impeccably pleated black smock. It makes him look like he's in mourning, even in girl's clothing, in a landscape whose every leaf seems in place for eternity. The stew they eat in each of the outlying farms smells the same as ever. On a tree-trunk is a tattered auction notice officially posted during a regime to be followed by one only slightly bloodier.

Flies die on the stickly ribbon hung from the ceiling. The rings on the coal stove burners fit into each other perfectly. The walls were a problem: which color would show the dirt least? They decided on ochre. In the bedrooms, all kinds of wood, from oak to Brazilian rosewood. The whisk of brooms and feather dusters can't keep the noise out. If it's really nice weather, they open the windows wide. The hands on the clock never stop. If you leaned out a window you'd see silhouettes carrying a briefcase or a tool, sometimes followed by a dog. Children stay indoors, wrapped in warm, well-made clothes with every button tight. You think you see a faint tremor on the horizon.

There are those who would like to have all catastrophes happen and be done with—so long as they're sure that afterwards all will be calm for a long time, with the finest hint of the eternal in the air. And, at most, once in a while, the dust of tragedy will rise from a broken column, a theatrical column that wouldn't look quite right. In this life of keeping up the old appearances you'd need to put up a good-natured front. The insects would still be there, multiform and well armored; there'd be plenty of time to study them, a drink, if you wanted one, close at hand. The hand would be wearing starched cuffs, like those on finely drawn hands you still find pointing the way down some small town hall's yellowed corridors. So it would be a life of happy bit players: docile dogs, cunning cats, comely housemaids, bakers, delivery boys, chimney-sweeps, cobblers, punctilious jewelers. "But wouldn't a life like that be despicable, even with all the spectacular sunsets it might entail?" you think, called back to the restlessness of days present.

During the summer 1910, an air show is put on at the city race-track. The posters for it were hung on barn doors. There's only going to be one plane, a single aviator, enough to be thrilling. Everyone, from town or country, dressed in Sunday best, turns out for the exhibition, the first of its kind at the county seat. The aviator wears an outfit like Blériot's. The cathedral spires are topped by this plane that a body of citizens, grocers, teachers, dignitaries takes off its hat to as the conquest of the century. Still, everything stays calm, pacified, like a tiny village in a glass ball, although peasant women in their starched costume unchanged since the Middle Ages raise their wrinkled heads, look at the monoplane, and softly pronounce the astonished and fearful interjection: Alas! alas!

For years on end a family may keep the hat a stranger, on a one-night visit and gone by dawn, left behind him. If the city comes to act out another drama, this bizarre hat will have a part. Elsewhere, an adjutant's silver epaulettes slung on a hook inside an armoire door are something of a relic. A billet brought the young officer to the house. He left so early the birds hadn't started to sing and no one was at the day's work. At length such objects disappear, with a slim chance of surfacing in the memory of an insomniac curled tight in bed in some downhearted district's last hotel.

In 1880, hair counts a lot in the impression women make; it can add to their attraction. In the morning, through a half opened window, you see those long falls of hair—black, auburn, brown, red, or blond—that make the woman look like some enchanted animal. Their hair spills all the way below the waist, to the place God reads as easily as the heart, according to the preacher. Straight-haired women envy those with naturally curly hair. They talk of it as if it were a private income. "Oh what thick wavy hair she's got," they say. Raising his head from time to time to see the morning sky glint or darken, the gardener tends his beds. His rake rasps along with the noise a comb makes in tufts full of static, coming to again after the languid night. The hair is slowly arranged in front of a bevelled dresser mirror as the smell of lilacs floats through the window. It takes concentration to get the hairpins right. There are days when strict buns refuse to be built up after you've unwoven the long braids made for those hours of sleep.

One evening at the turn of the century you see a mathematician reach home carrying a birdcage. Absent-minded as scholars will be, he took it without even noticing from a sidewalk display on the birdseller's quay. Threading his way through black and yellow hansoms, he didn't see the dog running down an alleyway with a leg of lamb in its mouth, or the furious, mustachioed butcher giving chase. In the future the memory of such ludicrous times will flicker. Citizens who have survived the massacres will be sitting on caned chairs, arms crossed, before their eyes the ghost of the professor all in black, his well-brushed cutaway, the uninhabited cage in his hand.

In houses one approaches carefully there are stairs to be climbed, once the door's open, before reaching the one room that's lived in. From below, the woman who's calling inquires, "Are you there?" And the woman who's up there alone answers, "Yes, I'm waiting for you to come up." The visitor takes off her clogs so she won't track in dirt. The wooden stairs groan under her weight. That's what it's like to go out in society: one has to observe unwritten rules of etiquette. When the two women are sitting face to face, they speak guardedly and their shadows almost touch on dead white walls. A vegetable aridity takes hold of the space around them: wicker breadbaskets, some other summer's nuts, yellowed bunches of beans hung up to go to seed. Nothing out of place.

At dinner, a civil sevant loses patience with badly cooked meat. Not with poisonous whirlwinds. His oldest son crumbles bread in his own peculiar dreamy fashion, and the mother declares, "He has his whole life in front of him." The boy senses his father's anger about to flare up at him at the end of the meal. It will be at the breaking point as he asks: "What will become of you?" The man's hands will move feverishly. There's a figurine on the mantle-piece, a bronze goddess. No one notices her bare breast. Her maker left the other one draped.

In the afternoon, one of the women goes up to her room to look at herself in the mirrored wardrobe door that creaks when you open it to hang something up. She pushes out her chest beneath a black dress the sunshine bites at.

The sound of wind revives the old days when bread and wine and even bread dunked in wine tasted different. A considerable amount of time has piled up. The numbers of certain years no longer evoke anything. A small girl appears blindfolded for blind-man's buff, an eternal figure. Several other girls run in a circle around her. Which one has tagged her? Once she's able to tug on a sunlit, uniquely braided pigtail, she guesses and then lets out a singular cry of pleasure which will never know an equal.

Schoolchildren holding hands pose for a photographer from the postcard company. Just then a bell tolls a passing: suffering has had its way with a proud body. For nights on end a cramped room would be light, dark, then light again; a tattered book lay there on a table. While the children, near a grey statue, stare at the lens, one branch of a rosebush quakes; it will be blurred in the photograph, but the children will show up clearly in their bulky clothes. Their faces have a modest look, susicious, already cruel, the town cynic might say.

If a child skins a knee in mock battles after school, parents don't worry too much about it. Teachers get back to their rooms with paperbound books. The day's end encourages the confidential talk of those fond of tête-à-têtes in the shadows. The conversation begins with the usual subjects and goes on, matched by brief birdcalls. One of them hears the clock mete out its strokes. "Is it already that late?" he exclaims. An excuse to escape, for no longer being contradicted. Silence has won ground. You no longer hear the scattered schoolchildren; everyone goes home, into himself.

"We're lost," the husband says to his wife in her flowered hat; they no longer know which way to go. The night comes on. Birds fall silent. They make a wild guess. A clearing turns up, a peasant woman sitting there gives them directions. They're saved. The countryside is full of life again: cows and mares are calm. "Let's hurry up," one of them says, "It's not getting any earlier." "I know, I know," the other replies. They come to houses at the edge of town. The windows are full of staring people saying nothing. For the couple this is a new kind of fear. They blanch and quicken their pace. So goes the story of their life.

A child's frail voice reads the battle of the Israelites and the Philistines. A woman in her nineties, whose three daughters died past the age of seventy, keeps saying: "It's a shame, I couldn't raise one of them." When the Jesuit back from China tells his mother the customs of the Mandarins, she replies: "Could be." She thinks the important thing is for him to keep his dead father's watch in his hidden cassock pocket. Smoking his pipe, pulling his black beard, he sees every crack in the plaster. Married women's hands do endless chores. Wallpaper flowers are tearing in places. A girl has got undressed, her body trembles with a soft sensation that hurts.

The middle-aged teacher lets his small son sit on his knees and push his head from left to right, right to left. The child, tired of the game, stops. But the father keeps swaying his head, says: "Well, now you've done it, it'll never stop going back and forth like this." The fear-stricken child shouts, "No," to break the spell. Then the man stops, makes everything return to normal: chairs, sideboard, floral patterns on the curtains, a half-drunk cup of oily coffee that he will finish only to knead a small ball of bread between index finger and thumb. In the garden, shrubs will twist in a sudden wind—the image of his life.

People try to fight time. A pet is a help. But the number of infinitesimal creatures populating a house—how could you ever count them? They occupy the grooves in the floor, the rafters; they settle from peak to foundation, even in the flour supply. If one of them walks on a windowpane, a slender index finger annihilates it: all of it goes under: respiratory and circulatory systems, sense organs. But it might, on the other hand, walking on the rim of a big heavy copper pot, drop into a thick brown sauce, die there like the worker who lost his step and fell into a vat of molten steel one starry night.

Insomniacs toss and turn in their beds, their minds pinned by the preposterous word, the relentless idea. They wish sleep would hit them like a brick. Some carry with them badly buried secrets; they know someone has killed, willfully or not. All the same, childhood appears with its candor, tricks, greed, awkwardness, its silly outfits with braided trim, its starched lace ruffles all the more out of place against this backdrop: full-grown trees in a sepia autumn.

The women say: "It looks like rain." The clouds burst, they all go inside and open the linen closet so they'll feel secure. Counting the sheets claims its due importance. On stormy days they'll comfort each other: "It won't hit us," one of them says, "there's the lightning rod at the school, and on the bank, and the cathedral. Oh, maybe if we lived a mile away, out in the open, but not here!" If a gale blows up while someone's visiting, they tell her as she leaves: "You can't be serious, you can't go home in this mess, it's impossible." So she stays, and her sweet face is livid that instant the sky lights up.

The house sits well back; the doors are open but no voice comes from it. It's often like that in the country. Then whoever's come back—a soldier on leave, a missionary back from the tropics, an unapprenticed boy—steps in. Dishes stay calm. The clock with stone weights is running. The village has moved to the fields. Solitude along the roads, looking east or west, but the hedgerows' each leaf gives its all against its death. Then the one who's back home pronounces the time-honored words: "Anybody here?" Every sign suggests he might as well admit there's no one there. It's true you can't sit down to wait in all this light.

A middle-aged man's wife tells him: "Put on your hat, you'll be cold." So he puts on his derby. It would take a long time to describe it, if you wanted to be exact: the band, the tight stitching at the brim that wears out faster than anything else, the white lining with the hat shop's name stamped in gold and rubbing off, the leather band inside with the wearer's monogram. During riots men wearing such hats were easy targets. They fell to the ground, their black hats rolling on the earth that was dry or cracked or sodden, or even covered with snow.

Alone at home now, the woman looks out the window, sees only a few trees and the sky.